I Stole God
· From ·
Goody
Two-Shoes

HEATHER◆HARPHAM

HARVEST HOUSE PUBLISHERS
Eugene, Oregon 97402

I STOLE GOD FROM GOODY TWO-SHOES

Copyright © 1994 by Heather Harpham
Illustrations copyright © by Steve Bjorkman
Published by Harvest House Publishers
Eugene, Oregon 97402

Library of Congress Cataloging-in-Publication Data

Harpham, Heather.
     I stole God from Goody Two-Shoes / Heather Harpham.
       p. cm.
     ISBN 1-56507-224-3
     1. Mothers—Religious life.   2. Wit and humor—Religious aspects—
Christianity.   I. Title.
BV4529.H33   1994   94-10727
242'.6431—dc20   CIP

Printed in the United States of America.

94 95 96 97 98 99 00 — 10 9 8 7 6 5 4 3 2 1

For Noah and Nathan

CONTENTS

Beyond Ordinary

Beyond Ordinary

This is a writer's favorite kind of book—one that's already written for the most part. Many of these pieces were first published in "Out of the Ordinary," my column in *Virtue* magazine. Others are current, or else rewritten for this book.

Often people ask me, "So, what do you write about?"

My answer always embarrasses me a little. "I write about myself," I have to say, "I write about my life."

But maybe I could also say, "I write about your life." So often my stories resemble yours, and your stories, mine. The way we experience life, God, our families, our dreams. We all need to identify with and connect with one another. And that's what this book is about—finding joy, humor, and meaning in our lives.

But this book also contains unexpected tragedy, another part of our stories. There's a chapter here I'd rather not include, a part I hate to tell. But it's also too large to leave out, and you may have lived it as well.

Years ago, I wrote, "Standing here in the mud, watching from a distance, I see my family more close up than ever."

That distance is no longer a pumpkin patch, but time gone by and change. Sometimes I miss the way we were. But I also sense that God is still watching us, near and far, then and now. And He loves us the way we are.

As you read these stories, I hope you, too, will see your friends and family more clearly than ever. And I hope you'll pause, stuck in mud perhaps, to notice God close up in your life. How He occupies your most ordinary moments. How He loves the way you are.

I Stole God
·From·
Goody
Two-Shoes

I Stole God
from Goody
Two-Shoes

THIS MORNING MY SISTER CALLED ME AND WE argued about God. But then, my sister and I have been fighting over God for as long as I can remember. That's how I first came to know Him. I sort of stole God from my sister when she wasn't looking.

Kathy was the first in our family to accept Christ. She was fourteen when she got involved with a youth group at a local church. After that, she played her guitar and sang songs about God day and night—or so it seemed to me.

Back then I imagined that I hated my sister—and her God. Once I barged into her room and tore all the Christian posters off her wall. Often we ended up in gruesome hair-pulling fights. Each would grab a fistful of the other's hair and then we'd both be screaming and crying until she let go (I always won).

Even though my sister was three years older, I was the tougher one, the bully. The nicer she acted, the meaner I became. She was vulnerable and good in a way I felt I could never be. So I took joy in stabbing at her soft spots.

The worst part of these fights was always afterward, when my sister apologized. She would crack open my door and say, "I still love you, Heather. I'm so sorry. Will you forgive me?"

And then I would say something like, "I can't believe it. You make me sick. Get out, Goody Two-Shoes!"

Our parents' divorce when I was six had left me bitter. For years, I had not only lashed out at Kathy, but at Mom, my stepdad, and other siblings. Finally I was banned from eating dinner with the rest of the family. I had to wait until they were done or else eat by myself in the dining room.

One night several weeks after this edict, I was standing in the kitchen near dinnertime. I'd been making my family laugh and they seemed to be liking me. They were all getting ready to sit at the table and so I decided to risk it . . . I casually joined them.

A few moments later, my stepdad glared at me and said, "What do you think you're doing?"

I flew up from the table, yelling something vengeful in return. I don't remember now if I cried, only that my sister did. I could hear her downstairs bawling on my behalf and saying, "How could you hurt her feelings like that?"

Around this same time, something or Someone began drawing me to my sister's room while she was gone. I secretly played her Christian records and read her Christian books. I was searching for the love I felt coming from her and for some sign of softness within myself.

I didn't want my sister to catch me sneaking some of her God and realize I was softer than she thought.

But I was always careful to put things back in their place. And I kept vigilant watch out the window for my sister's car to pull up in the drive. I didn't want her to catch me sneaking some of her God and realize I was softer than she thought.

Then one night during my freshman year, I crawled out of my window onto the roof that overlooked our neighborhood. I stared at the stars and began to sob and sob. I was tired of being tough; tired of fighting a losing battle. I cried out to my sister's God until He became mine.

Within a few months, I began professing my new faith to my friends in a cautious, nonchalant way. But I didn't talk about Him much at home. I had to be careful. I still had my pride, and I didn't want my sister to think I'd gotten God from her.

This morning when Kathy called, we continued our love-war over God. She is still the gentler one, and I am still stubborn and loud. She is guarded with her Christianity while I like to sit on rooftops and gaze over every ledge. Sometimes I think we still have a glob of each other's hair in our hands.

I admit it now. I stole God from my sister. And she says that when I snuck God from her, I only left more of Him behind. This morning we both grabbed hold of this unfathomable God we share. And we laughed as we wrestled, sure of one thing: Neither of us will ever let go.

CHAPTER TWO

All Things
Green and Good
for You

MANY THINGS IN LIFE ARE HARD. GETTING MY-self out of bed in the morning is hard. Getting my children *into* bed is even harder. However, neither of these things can compare with how hard it is to get my three-year-old to eat something green, textured, or even remotely resembling two of the four major food groups (meat and vegetables).

Don't get me wrong. I realize that I'm not the only mother in the country who's considered intravenous feeding. I've seen other little birds like mine in the past. I used to chuckle to myself at the way their mothers tried to cajole, coax, bribe, and finally threaten them to eat something besides Saltines.

I could laugh for two reasons. First of all, I couldn't understand what all the fuss was about. Why didn't these mothers just *make* their finicky children eat what was good for them? Obviously, they must've done something wrong, early on, for their children to have developed such an incredibly picky palate.

The second reason I could laugh is that my first child greatly misrepresented what "normal" children like to eat. His first word was "meeaat." And then in Sunday school when all the children were asked about their favorite foods, Noah announced his two top choices as broccoli and spare-ribs (all the other kids chose pizza, ice cream, and candy).

This left me ill-prepared for child number two, Nathan, who all but regurgitated the foods Noah had enjoyed. At first, I thought the problem could be solved if I were clever. I mixed in little pieces of vegetables or other healthful foods with things he liked. I did this while I thought he wasn't looking. "Thought" is the key word here. How did he know?

Later I was to discover that this sixth sense extended even beyond my tricks. I would appreciate it if one of these expert pediatricians or psychologists would tell me how a child can know, without ever tasting it, that butterscotch pudding is something good, but pretty orange squash is to be avoided at all cost?

Getting desperate, I at last turned to bribery. "Nathan, if you will be a good little boy and eat at least half of your dinner, I'll let you have some ice cream for dessert."

Sometimes this worked. An hour later, half his food was so played with and spilled on the table or floor, I'd call it good and give him the ice cream. Other times, the num-miness of the reward just couldn't compensate for the purportedly disgusting taste of dinner.

Today I no longer chuckle at frustrated mothers who try to give a child a bite of something ten times. I have compas-sion for other women who have to take tucks in all the pants they buy their children, or else purchase only coveralls which, though baggy, don't fall down every time Junior toddles off.

These days I watch such mothers carefully for clues I may have missed. Maybe there's a secret way to motivate children to eat beans I've never heard of. Usually, however, their child is no more reasonable than mine, and they are no more capable of force-feeding than I am.

In the end, we commiserate together, mutually amazed at how our little stick children manage to carry on such active lives with such a small amount of sustenance.

A lot of people say I worry too much about it. They say he'll eat what he needs. I guess maybe they're right. Maybe as Nathan gets older, he'll change. He'll start to love spinach and beg for seconds of roast beef. He'll give up crackers in favor of trail mix. Maybe he'll even want milk once in a while.

Then again, didn't God sustain the Israelites on manna and water alone? Maybe Nathan's getting food from heaven I don't know about. Or maybe a mother's love *is* a kind of manna—and as good as anything green.

CHAPTER THREE

The Only Thing I Ever Knew for Sure

THE FIRST TIME I LAID EYES ON MY HUSBAND HE was standing in the food line in our high school cafeteria, trying to look cool. His thumbs were casually hooked in his belt loops while he contemplated whether to buy three or four submarine sandwiches for lunch. A friend of mine nodded his way and whispered, "That's Tom Harpham."

As the only six-foot-three-inch freshman in our high school, Tom stood out. I remember taking in his looming frame, his longish hair, tie-dyed Rolling Stones T-shirt, and deciding he was the homeliest thing I'd ever seen.

Tom and I didn't start out with a lot in common. He was a good athlete with a reputation for getting into trouble. I was a good Christian girl with a reputation for staying out of it—or at least trying to.

Because the crowd I hung out with in high school was mostly non-Christian, I learned early on how to keep one foot in each world. Often I'd go to a party, drink beer, and then spend the rest of the night talking passionately about God to anyone who'd listen. Sometimes I'd gather a small audience. I can't remember now what points I made, beer in hand. All I knew for sure was that a God of love had sent

His Son to die for our sins. What I lacked in consistency, I made up for in sincerity.

Some of my friends were receptive. Sort of. One night a girlfriend and I had a particularly moving discussion about Jesus after she'd gotten drunk and been hanging her head over a toilet for hours. Being the only sober person present, I patted her back while she repeated over and over, "You were right, Heather. We're all sinners."

Another time I was at a party when several of us got into a discussion about the existence of God and Satan. It wasn't exactly an argument, but a couple of guys must have decided I was all wet. The next thing I knew I was being tossed, fully clothed, into the swimming pool.

*E*veryone laughed.
*Somebody got me a towel.
Nobody got saved.*

Everyone laughed. Somebody got me a towel. Nobody got saved. No wonder I hesitate to call either of these instances a witnessing success. And no wonder I'm nervous about seeing those people again. What happened or didn't happen in high school hasn't seemed important for years. But now suddenly it does, since our ten-year high school reunion is this August.

Yesterday afternoon, Tom and I sat on our porch swing and discussed our mutual reservations. Of course we will go, we agreed, but why does the idea of spending a weekend with these people scare us silly? Is it because we don't like who we used to be? Do we wish we'd been better examples?

I found part of the answer last night when I came across a great quote by Madeleine L'Engle. She said, "There is nothing so secular that it cannot be made sacred, and that is one of the deepest messages of the Incarnation."

Could it be? Could it be God was working despite my human failings?

Then I thought about my husband's baptism. It was a full immersion, clothes and all. I remembered how I cried freely as I sang choruses along with the rest of the small audience and how I kept hearing the echo of words I once said to my sister: "Tom will never come to God."

It struck me then that I'd been baptized twice. Once, like Tom, I was baptized into the family of God. But I also experienced a different kind of baptism. It was a full immersion conducted by my friends, fellow sinners—a sign that, though Christian, I was still one of them.

I'm still not sure what I'll say when I see them this August. We have a lot in common, which is a good place to start. But if given the chance, I'll end with the only thing I ever knew for sure, even back then. A God of love sent His Son to die for our sins.

Pray there'll be no pools.

CHAPTER FOUR

The Handsomest Man

TOM'S NEVER OWNED A SUIT IN HIS LIFE. IT NEVER mattered before—until now. For some time, he's been under consideration for a promotion at this part-time job with United Parcel Service. Last week it was finally time for the suit-and-tie interview with the district manager.

Like a lot of people, we've been battling a tight budget. But since the job would mean a pay raise, we decided this was an investment we had to make. Gulping down the price, we purchased a beautiful brown suit—wondering what we'd eat that week.

Tom also coaches basketball at a local high school part-time. The evening before the all-important interview, the team was scheduled to play its final game. The other coaches decided to wear suits and ties. Excited about finally having his own suit, my husband fussed over himself like a little boy.

"It does look pretty sharp, doesn't it?" He beamed. I thought he was the handsomest man alive.

When we pulled up at the school it was dark and raining. I was dropping Tom off so I could run errands and return later. I gave him a kiss for luck and told him once again how wonderful he looked. He headed quickly for the gym and I sighed with pride.

But as I prepared to leave, Nathan suddenly yelled, "Mommy, stop! Daddy's running after us!"

I stopped the car, thinking he must have forgotten something. He jumped inside and slammed the door; his face was flaming red. He looked angry.

"I fell!" he cried.

"You what?!" Then I saw it. A gaping tear in his pants. His scraped knee protruded through the huge hole. "Oh, Tom, no! You couldn't have!" I exclaimed. "How did you fall? You never fall! You've had that suit on for twenty minutes!"

For some selfish, unknown reason, I blamed him. Tom's outrage matched mine. He seemed ready to cry. "I'm not going in there," he gruffly informed me. "Let's go home."

"Tom," I reasoned, "you have to! At least go in and tell them you are going home to change clothes."

But he was too upset. A fallen man in a ripped suit must be something like a woman scorned. Rather than give him time to calm down and think clearly, I took matters into my own hands.

"Fine!" I flung at him. "Then I guess your wife will have to go in and explain for you. How stupid!"

I jumped out of the car and banged the door shut before he could protest.

I hurried toward the gym in the rain, bitterly convinced that I was woman on a mission for a complete klutz. I rounded a corner bordered by high shrubs—and then it happened. My cute boots escaped me and I slipped, falling so hard on the wet pavement that several bystanders rushed over in concern.

"That's so weird!" a woman said. "Someone else just fell down right here in this same spot a minute ago!"

"I know!" I cried, sobbing hysterically by now. "That was my husband!"

Finally I got to my feet, brushing away offers of assistance. I stumbled back to the car. When I climbed in, Tom realized there was something wrong—something more than his fall and our ensuing fight. He drove out of the parking lot before he asked me.

"I fell, too!" I yelled at him. "And I hurt my knees when I fell."

He looked back at me, obviously perplexed. We were a ways down the road before it really hit him. Before it hit both of us.

He began to smile first. "I fell!" he said. "And then you fell!" And then he started to laugh.

"I know," I said. "But I just can't understand how a grown man could just be walking along and fall!" I was still brushing back tears. "That suit cost so much money, and you've got your interview—"

And then I, too, began to shake my head and smile.

Once home, we mended our quarrel with laughter and forgiveness. We mended Tom's suit with an iron-on patch. It looked tacky. But he got the job, anyway. And I got God's point: Watch your step in the rain, because haughtiness really does go before a fall.

CHAPTER FIVE

The Truth About T-Ball

T-BALL IS A SIMPLIFIED VERSION OF BASEBALL. Even the name "T-ball" sounds simple. But words can be deceiving. And when Nathan played the game for the first time this summer, my husband and I discovered the sport was both more, and less, than it's cracked up to be.

At intervals throughout the first game, Coach Wanna-Win handed out intense discourses about how the outfield could make or break the team, how the infield must always know exactly where the play was, and how all of them had better move their feet and keep their eye on the ball. Just when the kids' faces were drawn into tight knots of concentration, he'd add, "Now remember to have fun!"

Some kids took his final advice—and that's all. They got interested in the game going on behind them. Or in the plane flying overhead, or in digging a hole in the ground with their toes. That, of course, didn't sit well with Coach Wanna-Win.

Tom and I observed it all quietly. And we patted ourselves on the back after each game for resisting our urges to razz the rotten ref, yell at Nathan when he missed a fly ball, or recommend to the ranting father sitting next to us that he buy himself a muzzle.

Just when we might get bored, something exciting would happen. Once, an infielder got belted right in the tummy by our son's ball. The poor kid doubled over in pain. All the men, including my husband, yelled congratulations to Nathan about what a good hit that was. All the mothers, including me, glared at the compassionless, competitive men.

Several coaches from the other team strode out to the mound and tried to soothe the kid, hoping he'd be tough. But inevitably, the player's dad appeared, picked up the blubbering boy, and with a hint of defensiveness carried him off the field.

Everybody clapped.

I didn't know her, but every time she struck out I felt it in my gut.

At this age, girls are allowed to play with the boys. The good thing about T-ball is that the ball is easier to hit when it's propped on a tee. The bad thing is that it's doubly humiliating when a kid still can't make contact.

I could tell Lacey concentrated with everything in her. Her blond hair tucked all up in her cap, her small arms poised and ready, she watched that ball—refuse to leave the tee. I didn't know her, but every time she struck out I felt it in my gut. When she cried, I put on my sunglasses so no one would know that I was about to, too.

Tournament time rolled around. The championship game, which would determine first and second place, was held at one o'clock in the afternoon in 95 degree weather. The kids probably sweated off five pounds in their frantic efforts. And Lacey finally figured out how to whack the ball. But our team lost anyway.

Later, while the sun beat down on the ceremonies, scores of proud parents watched to see their children receive a handshake and trophy. I was feeling impatient, sick of the heat, and crabby. And so I wasn't prepared for the lump that rose in my throat when our team took their turn.

Coach called out their names one by one. Ben, who always needed a kleenex. Chris, who always forgot to cover his base. Carl, who stumbled through the season wearing fifty pounds of catcher's equipment. Each one looked alternately embarrassed and thrilled as they accepted their trophy.

The solemn procession was almost over when it hit me. The truth about T-ball, that is. If you can forget the score long enough, it's packed with spiritual truths.

1. When you get blasted by another's ball, go ahead and cry. And then let your Father pick you up and carry you for a while.

2. When you strike out in life, remember there is probably someone on the sidelines wearing sunglasses who still believes in you.

3. When the coach of heaven calls you forward for your reward, forget how many errors you've made. There'll be no doubt in His mind: You're home safe.

CHAPTER SIX

Another Baby? The Great Debate

IT'S BEEN A FEW YEARS SINCE I HOSED DOWN A high chair that was shell-shocked from Food War II. By now, the sour smell of an overflowing diaper pail is only a faint, if fiendish, memory; and I've (almost) forgotten what it feels like to be bitten while nursing.

Nathan, my youngest, is starting kindergarten this fall and his big brother, Noah, will be in the third grade. This means I'm beginning to feel the first buds of newfound freedom. I see myself soaring far above playpens and teething pain forever. I catch an occasional glimpse of myself reading, relaxing, writing, or shopping 'til I'm dropping— instead of 'til the kids do.

But this also means something else. Just as I'm beginning to bask in this blessed absence of baby talk, I'm becoming a prime candidate in another arena. Every mother who has more babies than she has bathrooms is asking me, "Are you going to have a third child?" (Translation: Come keep me company in Gerberland.)

I used to answer this question easily. I'd smile and explain that when Tom and I first got married we decided to have four kids. After I gave birth to our first son, however, we felt compelled to drop that number to three. Once our second son was born, there could be no doubt—two would do nicely.

But lately, the confidence has left my voice when I say "no more children." I'm struggling with the difficult question almost every mother must face sooner or later: to have, or not to have another baby?

I have a friend who has two boys. She's emerged from this great debate in favor of Junior Number Three. But when she tallies the opinions, wanted and unwanted, of her husband, mother, and closest friend, here are the results: I say, "Go for it!"; her mom says, "Don't think so"; and hubby said, "Ain't no way!"

At least she and I agree. I say "yes" because for me, her having a baby would be almost as good as my having one. I could stop scaring myself silly even considering it.

So why am I? I'll tell you if you promise not to laugh. Long ago, I decided that I would have a daughter someday, and I would name her Hannah. Over the years, I've talked about her almost as if she already exists. Obviously, Noah and Nathan have cut in line in front of Hannah. Now I worry that she's floating around "up there" somewhere waiting to be born and asking, "What do you mean, you're not having any more children?"

I fear I'll get to heaven and God will say, "Heather, here is Hannah, your daughter you were too selfish to bear. . . ."

Of course, that's all silliness. And by now you're probably wondering why I don't just get pregnant and have Hannah. Several reasons: My greatest concern is that she'd turn out to be a Henry instead. This very thing happened to my sister who gave birth to baby Jonathan this month—her third boy who was supposed to be a girl.

Don't get me wrong. I love little boys. But I shudder at the thought of an additional piddler on the rim of my toilet, another child who won't let spiders or birds die in peace, and yet a third miniature man who wipes away my kisses just because of a little lipstick.

Besides, I have always wanted a daughter. I have imagined Hannah and me happily baking cookies side-by-side in the kitchen. I can already see us walking arm-in-arm amongst the glorious mobs of shoppers at midnight madness sales. I can almost hear her begging for my advice on boys, dating, and love.

I must confess, however, that I have doubts as well as dreams about Hannah. What if she demands to wear makeup at age eight and suffers from delusions of grandeur throughout adolescence? Horror of horrors, what if she acted like I did?

I shouldn't worry. So far, it looks as if my husband is intent on simply reproducing himself into blond, blue-eyed little boys. His genes are seemingly oblivious to the fact that I, with my dark eyes and hair, deserve equal representation in our children.

Meanwhile, I continue to weigh the odds and count the costs, keeping in mind that Hannah's not here to defend herself. If she were, she might remind me that the trauma a mother feels when her toddler throws her new shoe into the toilet or tosses a dozen eggs down the grocery store aisle is easily forgotten when that same child says, "I wuv you, Mommy."

She might try to tell me that the smell of a messy diaper is rarely as strong as the scent of a newborn's skin sponged clean and puffed with powder. She might even look into my eyes and ask, "Is the joy of an article sold or the solitude of a silent afternoon to be compared with the wonder of a giggly first step or a spontaneous peanut-butter-flavored kiss?"

Yes, there is much to weigh. But then again, maybe it's only a matter of time....

Hang in there, Hannah.

CHAPTER SEVEN

'Tis the Season

Five Revelations Put to Rest My Holiday Delusions

LAST YEAR'S CHRISTMAS SEASON BROUGHT THE usual: arm loads of presents, enough feasting to add at least two more ripples to each of my thighs and, of course, an overdrawn checking account. But it brought something new as well. I had revelations . . . revelations that put to rest forever my delusions about holiday gatherings filled with perfect people and perpetual merriment.

It began like every other year. Following a sticky six-hour car ride, my husband, our two boys, and I finally arrived at my mother's home feeling limp and exhausted. Tom went to unpack our suitcases and I joined in the kitchen duties.

We hadn't been there but an hour when it began to happen. My brother-in-law made a casual comment about my kids' behavior that scratched at my pride and I thought, "What exactly did he mean by that?"

A well-intentioned aunt proceeded to point out that, in her opinion, my youngest son was too skinny and she was just wondering: Do I feed him balanced meals?

That got my ire up and before long I was involved in a heated disagreement with my sister about how long to cook the potatoes. She wanted to boil them only fifteen minutes and I said twenty. She was so sure she was right. That's when I had Revelation No. 1: 'Tis the season to be rankled by relatives.

Moments later, my sister's kids come bawling into the kitchen to tattle on mine. I determined from their tearful tale that my boys were bent on tormenting them. Only a few hours earlier the boys had claimed they couldn't wait to see their *favorite* cousins!

I decided to call in their dad. And that's when I noticed he'd vanished. As my hunt for Tom progressed from room to room, I picked up steam. I finally found him huddled in a back corner of the house watching a football game on television. We ended up squabbling, and I had Revelation No. 2: Husbands already know about Revelation No. 1 and will go into hibernation to avoid it.

Our marital tiff, which we hid from the rest of the world, prompted my husband to emerge long enough to talk to the kids. I thought he was too bearish. I was wrong.

As soon as Big Bad Dad disappeared, the kids transferred their commotion into the kitchen, which was off-limits to them. They proceeded to whine and wail about how they were all starving and would surely die before 6 P.M. I was trying to talk above their clamor and re-explain my potato-cooking theory to my sister when I realized that my youngest son had been beating on my back with a Nerf sword yelling, "Mommy! Mommy! I got you!"

That's when I had Revelation No. 3: Children have no nerves—especially at family and holiday gatherings. But they have been granted special knowledge about how to get on ours.

Dinner was finally ready, and after a massive search of the house, we rounded up enough chairs so that all of the adults could sit together at one table. I'm not sure why we bothered. We ate Christmas Eve dinner with chunky mashed potatoes and in between bites we jumped up and down a dozen times each to attend the ten kids at the kids' table.

Before bed, each child opened one present which, as they predicted, contained a pair of dreaded, BOOOORING jammies. All of them loudly protested, "Why couldn't I open a toy?"

After everyone unappreciative and under age sixteen was bedded down, the grown-ups opened their gifts. I received things I'd always wanted—sort of. That's when I had Revelation No. 4: The people you see only on holidays don't really know you well enough to pick out presents for you. And there is still a spoiled child living somewhere inside of me.

Gift-giving ended around 11 P.M. As we began to head toward bed, my mother declared that the night was still young. Her church has a midnight candlelight service on Christmas Eve. Secretly none of us wanted to go. But Mom was singing in the choir and it meant so much to her, and that's what it's all about, she said, and of course we were all going, weren't we?

We arrived too late to get seats so we had to sit in a dark side room, kind of like the family of the deceased at a funeral. We couldn't see my mom, but my sister and I could easily pick out her voice and that gave us a case of the giggles.

When it came time to light the little candles we were holding, a glob of wax dripped on my dress and it seemed uproariously funny. Wasn't it just yesterday she and I were children doing this? Suddenly the potatoes didn't matter anymore.

Tom was sitting on my right, but we were still engaged in a stubborn standoff. As the service progressed, I studied my candle, noting how the yellow flame seemed to stretch itself toward the shadowed ceiling like a child on tiptoe. A deep organ pounded out "Silent Night," and I felt something inside of me soften. Then at the end, we all stood up and sang, "O Come Let Us Adore Him," and I really did.

While I was singing, I sneaked a glance at Tom, reached over, and took his hand. He understood. He squeezed my hand back, then turned and smiled at me. I couldn't help noticing how his candle flickered and danced in his blue eyes, and I had the sudden thought that he was a wonderful husband, after all.

That's when I had Revelation No. 5, the only one that really mattered: 'Tis the season to expect nothing, forgive everything, and love all.

CHAPTER EIGHT

Almost Six

MY YOUNGEST SON, NATHAN, ANTICIPATES HOLI-days long before they're near. In July he begins to chant "Jingle Bells," and in November he starts scribbling hearts (they look more like pumpkins) for next year's Valentine's Day. Birthdays, however, hold first place in his preoccupation with special occasions.

He's been begging, even demanding, to be five since a week after he turned four. Three months before his fifth birthday, when he asked me for the umpteenth time, "How many more days?" I finally resorted to showing him nine flashes of all ten fingers, explaining that he'd have to go to bed ninety more times before he'd be a five-year-old.

He never asked to see fingers again.

When the day finally arrived, we had a nice party with lots of friends, presents, and an ice-cream cake. Nathan tore into the packages in typical five-year-old fashion and then afterward proudly announced his age, FIVE, at least ten times to everyone there—just to be sure.

Perhaps he enjoyed himself too thoroughly. Or maybe it was the fact that his big brother will soon be eight. I shouldn't have been surprised, but I couldn't help but feel defeated when a few days after his party, he began asking me, "When will I be six?"

In a way, I understand. I, too, grew up with an older sibling and was preoccupied with the number of years we'd each been alive. I considered the fact that I could *never* catch up to my sister a cruel curse.

But time changes things. I am no longer waiting, excitement in my eyes, to get a year older—and neither is she. I am also no longer a child dying to be an adult so I can do anything I want.

After all, we are grown-ups. We can do whatever we want!

All kids dream that dream, you know. It's what drives five-year-olds to obsession about becoming six. And it is why children everywhere can't understand why Mom and Dad don't eat candy bars all day, why we don't just paint the house purple, or stay up until 3 A.M. After all, we are grown-ups. We can do whatever we want!

In light of this dream, it's easy to understand why our kids question everything we say, and consider us obstacles to their very happiness. No wonder they insist on wearing high heels at age eight, and try to drive the car at twelve. They are grasping, fighting, trying to force that freedom day.

But it never comes. Not really. Because by the time they can finally drive a car, they will have to think about working so they can pay for that car, put gas in that car, and buy insurance for that car. By the time they are old enough to stay up as late as they want, they will feel pain the next morning at 6 A.M. when the alarm goes off.

And so the dream dies a gradual death as kids near adulthood. They realize that there's a reason Mom and Dad don't drive 100 m.p.h. down the highway. And they begin to grasp that even if their parents wanted to paint the house purple, the neighbors would rise up and attack.

This is why our kids don't *really* want to become like all the boring adults they know. They want to be free as a kid by the time they're like us. Buck the system. Do a new thing.

I got a preview yesterday when Nathan came bounding upstairs yelling happily that he'd decorated the table for Easter (two months away).

Hmmmmm, I thought as he led me with his grubby little hand through the kitchen. There it was, my child's idea of pretty: pink gum wrappers attached with huge globs of black electrician's tape all around the edge of our dining room table.

I gasped at first and then I caught myself. "Boy, isn't that nice, Nathan? How did you ever think of that?"

I didn't make a move to change his decorations for several days. Visitors to our home winced and stared. I didn't explain unless they asked.

Nathan? He felt proud of his project for days . . . almost grown-up, almost six years old.

CHAPTER NINE

Mother
Never Told
Me

THE OTHER DAY I STOOD FOREVER IN THE WRAP-ping paper section of the grocery store trying to select a Mother's Day card. I would pick one up, read the first two lines, choke on the sap, and replace it. Don't the people who write these cards realize that most of us grew up in the same house with our mothers?

I had a good mom. But she didn't dry every tear I shed, shine like a beacon in my darkest hours, and spend her every waking moment trying to add that "special touch" to our family.

Far from being pink, flowered, and pressed neatly into a card, Mom wore an aged pea-green bathrobe and often spoke anything but poetic lines. I remember when she was haggard and crabby and when she ran through the house slamming doors and crying that "nobody cares."

I recall these things now more than ever. Perhaps that's because I've joined her in the Mother World where children don't care if Dobson said it would work and where toddlers delight in demolishing tidy rooms just before company comes. I too have screamed on occasion, "Nobody cares!" And sometimes I've even believed it for a little while.

Of course, I didn't know it would be like this. No mother ever really does, or children might become an endangered species. I started out like most moms do—in pursuit of an ideal. I read up on parenting, studied the Bible, and aspired to become like the woman in Proverbs 31.

I was careful to teach my children about God, His goodness, His love for all creatures. And then, just when I thought my kids might be turning out to be sensitive, loving little boys, I found them on the back patio with a magnifying glass frying ants to death in the hot sun.

I tried to love my children unconditionally, imagining my devotion for them would never wane. But then the feelings sometimes did—especially when their hair got too long and scraggly. After they got it cut and came home all cute and clean-looking, I'd feel guilty about how much more I liked them.

*I realized
that someday my own kids
would grow old trying to pick out
a Mother's Day card for me.*

One day as I was busily picking something unrecognizable out of my carpet, I found myself resenting the fact that she, the Proverbs 31 woman, never had children who chewed bubble gum. Her kids probably didn't scribble on her furniture with Magic Markers either, I thought with a huff, so it's no wonder she could laugh at the days to come.

I began to doubt that my children would ever rise up and call me blessed, although they often rise up and call me mean. The truth sank in that I was failing. And I realized that someday my own kids would grow old standing in a Hallmark shop trying to pick out a Mother's Day card for me. I was contemplating such future glory one afternoon recently when I thought I heard God chime in with a TV commercial, "It doesn't get any better than this...."

"What on earth do You mean?" I asked, gazing around me at the commotion, messes, and what I assumed to be catsup on the kitchen wall. Gradually it dawned on me. God was trying to tell me I was normal, an okay mom, the "real thing."

But what about the gap?" I protested. "What about the gap between me and the Proverbs 31 woman?"

Then I saw that it was Him, laying down His life, connecting the "real" and the "ideal" forever. I recalled how God delights in processes, how He laughs with me, and I began to have hope.

That must be why I finally picked out a card for my mom that flowered and frilled, mushed and gushed, and basically called her "blessed." After all, she was a real mom in pursuit of an ideal, too. And now I know how close she really came.

CHAPTER TEN

The Grace
of a Goof

I KEEP A PICTURE OF JIMMY ON MY BULLETIN board. He looks the way I best remember him, about nine years old. His cowlick is sticking up, glasses sit crooked on his nose, and expression says clearly, "I'm a goof—and proud of it."

As it turns out, my little brother is not only still a goof, he's a would-be obstetrician as well. This morning, he called me before daylight to announce: "Our new baby girl just came into the world, sis. We named her Grace."

"Congratulations, Jimmy," I yawned. Actually, I didn't find the news too titillating. It may have been the hour. It may have been that this was their fourth child in the last five years and my sixteenth niece or nephew born in the last ten years.

"So how long was the labor?" I asked. We women like to compare notes on this. Anything less than a respectable eight hours is considered criminal.

"It was less than an hour," he said. "Just a few pushes and she was out."

I gasped. "How big was the baby?" Often this evens things out.

"Nine pounds, eleven ounces," he said.

Aha. "So how did she manage to deliver so fast?"

And then Jimmy, my little brother who couldn't eat with his mouth closed, who had watched 1,000 too many reruns of "Gilligan's Island" and didn't know what girls were until he was eighteen, said calmly, "I delivered the baby all by myself."

He went on to describe the process in great detail, how he tried to get help. He called the midwife. He called the next-door neighbor. He begged Tami not to push. But then the head appeared....

How could Jimmy expect me to believe a word of this? I remember him at ten, sitting across the table from me, making strange sounds. He used to repeat over and over again in a gravelly, irritating voice, "schnicker, schnicker, schnicker."

"Yeah," he continued, "and there's something else I'm proud of—I could see that the skin was stretching too much. She was going to tear—"

"Stop!" I wanted to yell. "I'm your sister who was careful not to let you see my underwear. You can't talk about these things. You shouldn't even know this. You're only four feet tall. I think I'm going to have to tell Mom—"

"And so," he said, "I applied pressure with my hand and pushed against the skin to keep her from ripping. And when the midwife got here she told me I did it exactly right."

"And the umbilical cord?" I ventured.

"Tami thought I was going to twist it right off."

Aha. Now this sounded more like Jimmy.

He always liked to fix things, change them. Once, he cut off the top of his car with a hacksaw. It was a Cutlass. He wanted a convertible. In the summer, you couldn't tell the folded top couldn't be raised. But in winter, he looked less than cool driving around town wearing a ski mask and gloves.

After we hung up, I prayed for Jimmy's new baby. I thanked God that Grace entered the world so easily and by her father's own hand. Maybe someday I'll explain to her that she was really delivered by a small boy with greasy fingernails who liked to make rude noises with his armpit.

But she probably won't believe me. Today, everyone calls her dad Jim instead of Jimmy. Except me. He writes computer programs, gets contracts from large companies, and manages other employees. The amazing part is he never went to college and we didn't even have a computer in our home. I guess some things just come naturally. Like go-cart savvy. Like goofiness all grown up. Like grace that arrives before you're ready and just won't wait to be born.

CHAPTER ELEVEN

God Has a Cellular Phone

MY HUSBAND'S JOB TOOK HIM TO MISSOURI FOR three weeks. I have missed his hugs, his warm body in bed next to me, his taking out the garbage. But yesterday I missed him most of all.

Tom is the one who watches the gas gauge and makes sure our van's tank is always full. This weekend the kids and I drove to visit relatives in Washington—and we attempted the trip, 350 miles each way, on one tank. Since I had no intention of ever refueling, it would have happened sooner or later. I just wish it would have happened somewhere else. We crawled to a stop on Interstate 5 north of Seattle on a bridge-like overpass with almost no shoulder.

"What are we going to do now, Mom?" the boys asked in scared voices.

Why were they looking at me? I was ready to start crying myself. It was all I could do not to turn to Noah, proclaim him the man of the family, and beg him to think of something.

Finally, I scribbled my mother's phone number on a piece of paper and crawled out the passenger side. I stood behind the van with the slip of paper in my hand, cars whizzing past. I felt so foolish. I couldn't even bring myself to actually flag someone down. So I simply tried to appear forlorn.

Meanwhile, I imagined how God might rescue me. I remembered angel stories I'd heard of in such situations. Or rare opportunities to witness. But really all I hoped for was a kind old man. Or better yet, a fellow female who would empathize.

After a half hour of trucks blowing past and debris flying in my hair, I realized I must not be good at forlorn. And when help finally did arrive, it didn't look at all like I thought it would.

My rescuers were three Arab men, wearing silk pants and lots of gold jewelry. They didn't even speak English.

"I'm out of gas!" I yelled over the traffic and wind.

One of the men went back to their car. *Aha!* I thought. *He must have a can of gas.* But he came back instead with a phone in his hand. Soon I heard my sister's voice on the other end.

"I am out of gas on I-5 where there is no shoulder," I wailed. "Send someone to save me!"

I didn't try to witness to the men. Instead, I thanked them profusely and tried to give them money for the phone call. But they refused, grinned large, white-toothed smiles, climbed in their luxury car, and drove off.

My stepdad finally showed up with gas. A policeman came, too, and helped direct traffic around us. But later it was the Arabs I kept thinking of. What made them stop? I considered all of our differences: race, religion, sex, occupation. All we had in common was our humanity. But that had been enough.

We got home late last night. This morning I am trying to ignore the still-unpacked suitcases so I can write my Christmas column. I thought I'd talk about gifts of wise men or Incarnation—not running out of gas.

> *God doesn't always look like a baby in hay, a king with a crown...or even a Savior in thorns.*

And then I realize I am talking about Christmas, after all. Because God was willing to become human, to appear foolish, I see a little of me and a little of Him in every person I meet. God doesn't always look like a baby in hay, a king with a crown...or even a Savior in thorns.

Sometimes He looks like three Arab men with gold jewelry, silk pants, and a cellular phone. He looks like a young policeman, too kindhearted to give this mom a ticket. He looks like my stepfather, edging out of his truck onto the busy highway, a gas can in his hand.

In two weeks, my husband comes home. I will hug him and cry and say, "I'm so glad to see you!"

Maybe I won't tell him I ran out of gas. Maybe I'll just tell him God saved me again—when I was stranded in a place where there was no shoulder but His.

CHAPTER TWELVE

Shopping Beyond Dropping

THE OTHER DAY, WE DID IT AGAIN. MY BEST FRIEND, Kim, and I packed up our four boys (two each—who says God isn't fair?), and headed for the shopping mall. The occasion? An emergency. The following day was my husband's company picnic, and my last year's swimsuit had not only balled up, but a small gauzy window of sorts had formed in the bottom.

Kim came along because she understands that picking out a swimsuit without your best friend is like picking out a wedding dress without your mother. (And because she can't resist any legitimate reason to surround herself with price tags and clothes racks.)

Unfortunately, it wasn't one of our more successful shopping trips. The makers of swimwear obviously don't know the difference between skimpy and obscene. And the boys . . . well, they were a little less enthusiastic than their mothers. They looked as if they'd rather be getting shots.

Kim and I torture ourselves like this quite often—often enough so that at some stores the clerks remove any displays from their counters when they see our children coming.

And often enough so that our husbands hide all the sale circulars that come to the house.

Don't misunderstand. It isn't that either one of us has a lot of money to spend. Often we're broke. But when that happens, there's always window-shopping and layaway. And don't forget there's always *something* lying around the house that just has to be returned or exchanged.

Of course, we don't always take all four boys. Whenever possible we try to have only one each. Even then, mishaps may happen. One time my then three-year-old, Nathan, mistook a near-empty clothes rack for a jungle gym. When it fell over everyone in the store wandered over to see who the fool mother was (as if something like this never had, and never would, happen to them).

Fortunately, Nathan was okay, but I had a hard time forgiving Kim for how she nonchalantly distanced herself from me—the woman with the monkey.

There've been times when I've thought to myself, "Are Kim and I insane or what?" But it was only a temporary thought, entering my mind somewhere between the promised trip to the pet store to see fishies and the fifth trip to the potty.

By now you're probably feeling sorry for our sons. Don't bother. I think in a subtle way, shopping with mom is preparing them to be good husbands when they grow up. Maybe when their wife makes the deal of the century, they'll appreciate it. And if she doesn't like to shop, just think how much they'll adore her!

I understand there *are* actually women out there who truly don't enjoy shopping. Can you imagine that?!

Maybe the reason some women don't like to shop is because they've never gone with a best friend. Without a best friend, who is there to tell you what looks good on you, and what makes you look like you've been embalmed? Who is there to help you justify, rationalize, and rearrange your grocery budget to buy that dress?

A couple of times, Kim and I have snuck away for an evening of childless shopping. Several weeks back, we had a particularly memorable time. We spent four full hours doing moonlight madness sales, fighting our way through mobs of competitive shoppers like ourselves—and enjoying every minute of it!

I never had to apologize to strangers for Nathan bursting through the wrong dressing room doors. No shrill and desperate voices pleaded for one last chance to be good and get a treat. And there were no quarrels about who gets to ride in the cart, push the elevator button, or play with the metal device for measuring shoe size.

For the most part, our husbands don't mind our shopping. They understand that a "take an additional 50 percent off sale" is cause for more excitement than we'll probably ever demonstrate in bed. They're relieved we beeline for the clearance racks instead of the new arrivals. But, most of all, I think they'll continue to smile at us and let us carry on . . . as long as we don't make them come with us.

Meanwhile, Kim and I are praying for daughters.

CHAPTER THIRTEEN

More
Sure of Love
Than Ever

LAST YEAR ON VALENTINE'S DAY, MY HUSBAND forgot me. He didn't surprise me with a bouquet, card, or even those gross chocolates with the creams in the middle—the ones that he forgets I hate.

Tom realized his mistake shortly before bed and apologized. He'd had an unusually hectic week at work. I insisted it didn't matter. But that's not what I was really thinking. Inside, I pouted about how little he must love me and how Valentine's Day makes so many wives and girlfriends miserable.

> *I* beg God
> to show me again what
> love is and remind me
> once more of what it isn't.

I wasn't fond of the cupid holiday even back in grade school. I remember carefully counting my Valentines in tiny white envelopes, worried someone had left me out. Sometimes I'd try to read a veiled message of devotion into a certain card a boy gave me, until I realized he'd given twelve other girls in the room the same card.

I like to think I've grown up a lot since then. That I'm no longer hung up on fifty-cent displays of affection. Surely by now I understand the true meaning of love. But do I?

Ten Valentine's Days have come and gone since Tom and I said "I do." He's been pretty good about cards and such. But in between holidays it's often shocked me to think the whole reason we live in the same house, eat our meals at the same table, and raise two kids together is because we're supposed to be in love.

I confess that at times our love has felt lost to me, and I've yearned for another kind of feeling. One with the thrills and uncertainties of second grade, the agonies and ecstasies of adolescence.

During such seasons, I chide myself and wonder if the mystery of love is one that I will ever solve. Then I beg God to show me again what love is and remind me once more of what it isn't.

Common sense tells me it's not found in movies where men love women who wake up mornings with makeup intact (Tom would have left me long ago). And I doubt the longevity of feelings I hear in songs on the radio. Yet, I'm convinced love has little to do with settling for the mundane in marriage.

Like many couples, Tom and I included a reading of 1 Corinthians 13 in our wedding. Anticipating our anniversary, I recently read the passage through again: Love is patient, kind, persevering. Never boasting, never proud. Hopes all things. Endures all things.

I laid aside my Bible and stared out our bedroom window at my husband in the front yard. He was shoveling snow off our walkway. Tom saw me in the window and stopped to wave. I waved back. Then he tipped his head to one side as if to ask why I was watching him.

I hadn't planned to, but I mouthed, "I love you."

My husband seemed glad. He was still smiling as he went back to shoveling snow.

Perhaps Tom and I are slowly unraveling this mystery together, without even realizing it. Maybe love is simply what's left after all the counterfeits and selfishness are stripped away. Maybe love can't truly be found until it's felt a little lost.

This Valentine's Day, I hope to recognize love whether it arrives in a bouquet of flowers that I worry cost too much or in the form of another apology.

Then again, instead of waiting for love to come to me, I suppose I could always chase it down. I could write Tom a note signed with our names in a heart. I could play tag with him out in the snow—and let him catch me.

I look out the window again. As I watch my husband still struggling to clear a path to the street, I feel more sure of this than ever: For those who never stop searching for it, hurting over it, and sacrificing for it, love waits to be found.

CHAPTER FOURTEEN

People Call It Camping

EVERY YEAR AROUND JUNE ALL MY FRIENDS START talking about the fun they'll have camping with their kids over summer vacation. And every year around June I begin frantically checking into the campaign for year-round school.

I confess. I have a bad attitude about one of America's all-time favorite family activities.

Correct me if I'm wrong, but isn't there something inherently insane about packing up half your house only to unpack it again for a few days in mosquito-infested woods, only to pack it back up again so you can take it home only to unpack it all over again?

I used to think my aversion to camping was something carried over from childhood. My only camping memory is of the time our family got lost, arrived at a park in total darkness, and set up our leaky tent by a lake just in time for a monsoon.

But since becoming a parent, I've tried to change my attitude for the sake of my kids. Just last summer I planned a spur-of-the-moment camping trip. It would be our family's first go-it-alone adventure.

I spent all day Friday, one of the hottest of the summer, packing up our van. I was a martyr, a saint. I hunted the storage room, I ravaged the garage. My two boys followed me around in amazement, alternately exclaiming to one another, "We're going camping!"

When my husband got home, he looked impressed, thanked me for my effort, and proceeded to pack the entire van all over again—properly. We squabbled a bit, rounded up the kids, and took off. We were destined for a good time. We were doing it, the all-American family thing.

An hour down the road, the boys realized they hadn't eaten dinner yet and became convinced they'd surely starve before we reached camp. We had plenty of food. But my husband had repacked it beneath the tent and bikes and sleeping bags and surely it'd be too hard to reload it all properly . . .

So we stopped at McDonald's. A half hour later, we were back on the road. Our spirits lifted. We were going camping! We had several sites in mind. We drove to the first one, a well-known spot. It was full. "Too bad you guys weren't here about fifteen minutes ago," said the ranger. So much for fast food.

We drove on. The kids got a little antsy. When will we be there? Park number two. Full. It was getting dark now. We had one last place in mind. It was a bit of a drive, but we decided to risk it.

We were in luck! The attendant said he thought there was a spot still available. We drove through the grounds, locating the last vacant site in time to watch a smug-looking elderly couple with a fancy mobile home whip into it.

Don't misunderstand. There were other camping sites, all up and down the highway—if you didn't care about bathroom facilities, running water, a picnic table, a trail, or any recreational outlets. If you wanted a place to park your car, make yourself dirty and miserable and bored, and sleep on bumpy pine needles and rocks, there were lots of spots.

We arrived home around 1 A.M. The boys had fallen asleep in the car, flashlights in hand. We carried them in, thankful their entire world wouldn't fall apart until they awoke in their own beds tomorrow morning. Amazingly, it didn't hit them until they were on their second bowl of cereal that they were supposed to be in the woods somewhere.

Tom and I thought about being coy. "Sure we went camping! Don't you boys remember?" We'd say this with serious faces. "Yaaah. We roasted marshmallows, Noah, and you burned yours. We went swimming and fishing. Remember that huge fish you caught, Nathan? Too bad we had to let it go..."

It's not hard to guess how I spent my Saturday. Unpacking. In the heat. Putting away the lantern I'd finally located. The stakes to the tent I'd almost forgotten. The sleeping bag I worried Nathan might have wet last time he slept at a friend's.

Actually, the boys didn't take it as hard as I thought they would. Maybe it was because we pitched our tent in the yard for them to sleep in that night. Or maybe it was because of the promise we made them. A promise I'm worried they haven't forgotten. A promise I'm scared we'll have to keep this summer.

Please, somebody, save us a spot!

CHAPTER FIFTEEN

Chasing Life's Best Dreams

NATHAN ANNOUNCED HIS LIFE'S GOAL THE OTHER morning. Wants to be an artist. This happens to be the twentieth "when I grow up" occupation he's pledged himself to in the last six months. And I worry for him that he won't be able to squeeze out Mona Lisas in between being a doctor, a policeman, and an ice-cream-truck driver.

Although I doubt that all of Nathan's dreams can come true, I find myself encouraging every one of them. And in the process, I'm learning that even high praise has its hazards—like the other day when Nathan proudly presented me with a drawing of myself that looked more like a twisted tree.

"Nathan!" I exclaimed. "That's good! You're turning out to be quite an artist."

"What's an artist again?" he asked.

"An artist is someone who draws or paints pictures and then sells them to people," I explained.

Nathan disappeared into his room. Ten minutes later he reappeared wearing his coat, with his fist full of scrolled papers. "I'm going out now, Mom!" he yelled as he darted for the door.

"Where?" I asked, surprised.

"Around the block to sell my pictures," he said simply.

That was a hard one. I didn't want to crush his dream. . . .

I remember when my first dream, that of being a writer, was temporarily smashed. My sixth-grade teacher had led me to believe I was a budding word genius. But when I got into seventh grade, the English teacher was so absorbed in alternately drinking coffee and applying fresh orange lipstick that she didn't notice my literary knack. I threw in my pen and didn't pick it up again for years.

Of course, not every dream a kid dreams is feasible. My husband recalls how he and his childhood buddy made a pact that one day they would share an apartment with their football hero, Fran Tarkenton. "At the time, it seemed so possible, almost inevitable," says my husband wistfully.

Fran, where are you?

My older son, Noah, doesn't seem to dream dreams—or at least he won't admit to them. But he does dawdle over books about space and ask questions about astronauts. And then the other day at his baseball game he hit a home run. He finished running the bases with a flushed face, sparkling eyes, and, I'm almost sure, a dream.

I sat on the sidelines and rooted for both the dream and the run. And that got me wondering: Why do some people chase their dreams and others don't? Why do some dreams die while others live on?

I grew up with a girlfriend, Diane, who wanted to be a nurse. When we were twelve we both got our first bras and, feeling very grown up, our first dreams. We spent hours lying in her backyard, planning and plotting about how someday she would save people's lives, and I would write books.

Diane stayed determined about becoming a nurse. I lost touch with her after high school and didn't see her again for several years. When we finally did run into each other, she informed me that she was, in fact, a registered nurse. I rejoiced for her—and then I started writing harder.

There was another dream, however, that Diane and I once shared. We both attended church camps during the summers of our adolescence. Sitting around campfires and singing songs like "It Only Takes a Spark," we came to know God. And we made solemn, if vague, spiritual vows about how we'd both love the Lord forever.

But when Diane and I were exchanging the details of our lives, she didn't mention Him—even when I did. She seemed to squirm when I reminded her about that dream. I wondered if it got snuffed out by some tragedy; or did it just flicker and die slowly for lack of oxygen? I questioned myself about whether one dream fulfilled will be enough for her. And I cried because I know it won't.

I ended up telling my amateur artist that he could go door-to-door after all—but he'd have to give his dreams away for free. As I watched him scurry off, I prayed a prayer. Not that all of his dreams would come true, but only the ones that really matter.

CHAPTER SIXTEEN

It's Hard to Be Good

FOR KYLE, BEING TWO YEARS OLD WAS MERELY basic training in terror tactics. Now that he has perfected impishness, he is demolishing the myth of the "terrible twos" and erecting, among mothers who know him, a dread of the traumatic threes.

Kyle is my friend Debi's three-year-old. The other day she asked me to babysit him. I took a deep breath, and in a fraction of a second I weighed the value of our friendship. Debi is a great friend, and so I said a hesitant "yes."

Kyle did pretty well—until lunchtime. I told him he'd have to eat at least half his meal before he'd get any cookies. He proceeded to rearrange the food on his plate a hundred different ways. He splattered it, flew it around in circles in the air, and then landed it.

Tired of his show, I ran upstairs to sort some laundry. When I came back down, Kyle's plate was unchanged, his seat empty. I found him squatted underneath the table, his face smeared with chocolate, his cheeks bulged out with stolen cookies. He shook his head and mumbled, "I didn't eat no cookies."

For some reason, I didn't believe him. And I stood there staring at him and thinking how far some of us will go to avoid the truth.

A few weeks ago my sister's son asked her if he could remove a large rock from the rockery that lines their driveway. "Of course not, Adam!" she said. "That would ruin the landscaping."

Later she peered out her kitchen window at an obvious gaping hole in the rockbeds. Adam's defense: "I didn't pull it out! I only pulled out all the little rocks around it—and then the big one fell out by itself!"

My sister was stumped. To punish or not to punish? I sympathized with her dilemma, and together we reminisced about how our own mother had never seemed stumped. When in doubt, she always went for the hairbrush.

My brother used to run from my brush-wielding mother. She'd chase him through the house, up and over furniture, behind the piano where he couldn't squeeze. "How many? How many?" he'd bawl. Of course, the longer it took her to capture him, the more he got.

I, on the other hand, prided myself on taking my punishment bravely. I'd bend over and let her swat me, then I'd smile up at her and say, "That didn't hurt a bit!"

God has shown great mercy to me so far, since my own boys haven't as yet succumbed to such sarcasm. Although, when Noah was small, he came close. When I'd tell him, "You come here," he'd shuffle his feet toward me so slowly that movement was hardly perceptible.

There were times I broke down and laughed at him. Just like the other day with Kyle. I couldn't keep back a smile.

But I didn't mention my blunder to Debi, for fear she'd think I'd ruined her kid's concept of right and wrong.

That night, my Scripture reading included a proverb about God's discipline. I pondered whether God is ever tempted to chuckle at us. And I thought about how, in many ways, I am still so much a child in my response to Him—and to sin. Sometimes, I run away. Sometimes, like Kyle, I pretend not to know.

Lately, I can identify with Adam. I find myself standing in front of my own bed of rockery. I've already pulled out a few small stones, trying to get at the big one in the middle, almost afraid I might succeed.

Debi is trying to help me resist. We go for long walks and we talk. She reminds me that disobedience doesn't pay. And because I don't want to end up under the table, my mouth stuffed full of sin, I am listening to her.

Often I sense that God is watching, hoping I'll do what's right. And with a rush of reassurance, I realize He understands the temptations all of us feel. He knows how we hurt. He knows where we hide. But He also knows how to help. And hairbrush or chuckle aside, His discipline is love.

CHAPTER SEVENTEEN

Inside
the Closet
of PMS

I USED TO INSIST I DIDN'T HAVE IT. I TRIED NOT TO even consider the possibility. But that's hard to do when so many articles in your favorite magazines are about coping with PMS. And every other commercial on TV depicts a white-faced, bloated woman stumbling through a maze of hormones in search of a pill to cure it all.

It also doesn't help that most of my friends are "calendar keepers." These are women who religiously mark those special days with huge black X's. They keep better track of these X's than of their doctor appointments or relatives' birthdays. And they always speak of their cycles in terms of the four seasons.

Fall is the traditional bloated week-prior, when a woman feels like a walking waterbed. Winter is the "week of the X's" when she and her husband or toddler have who-can-be-the-crabbiest contests. In the spring, a woman should be snapping out of it. Summer, it turns out, is the only safe or happy week of the month. (No wonder these women are irritable!)

I used to think I was the only woman alive who didn't claim to suffer PMS. But that was before the other night at

Bunko. Bunko is a game where a dozen emotionally unstable women at various points in their cycles get together and roll dice for prizes. (Bridge has become far too complex for women in this day and age of PMS.)

Anyway, one of the women playing must have been heading into her fall. Because she started talking about PMS and crabbiness. The rest of the women around the table all nodded with sympathy—except for one lady who announced brightly, "Oh, I don't have that problem!"

I think that was the first time I saw it. How dangerous denial could be.

I was about to nod in agreement, when everyone stopped talking, and through strained smiles and barely veiled glares they congratulated the non-sufferer.

About five minutes later, this same lady lost a big round in the game. She came unglued. She insisted that she'd rolled her dice before the bell rang. She threw her pen onto the table, stomped over to the food tray, and began to down brownies in huge mouthfuls.

The other women looked surprised, and then relieved. "Face it, lady," they told her gently. "You've got it good. You've got it bad. It's PMS for sure. And since we see you're in the winter of your cycle, we'll forgive your little outburst."

I think that was the first time I saw it. How dangerous denial could be.

I went home pouting because I didn't win a prize. I slammed the front door, and when my husband asked if I'd had fun—I bit his head off. I told my crying son that I'd make all of his imagined nightmares come true if he didn't get back in bed. And then I ran upstairs and did some calculating.

Sure enough. It was PMS.

I'm glad I finally came out of the closet. I would have sooner if I'd known how much this syndrome accounted for. Now when I break down and start bawling because I can't find the lid to my favorite Tupperware bowl, I can reassure Tom that I'm simply heading into my winter.

Speaking of husbands, I feel sorry for them. The other night mine announced that his life is one-third over, and I could tell by the way he sat slumped on the couch that he was depressed. I wanted to ask him what season he was in . . . and then I remembered the poor guy has no cycle to blame.

But I'm not sure Tom would appreciate it even if he had one. You should have seen the look on his face when I told him a lady in town is starting a PMS support group out of her home. He wondered whether they'll plan the meetings around their cycles—and if they don't, how long they'll last.

Men.

None of this is to imply that women don't *truly* suffer. For many women, PMS is no laughing matter. Either way, I agree that there are some things some women just shouldn't do while under the influence. I try to avoid writing, for example. It seems during that week in the fall, I have all the spiritual depth of a prime-time game show host.

That reminds me. What day is it today? What have I been saying?

Oh well. Maybe it doesn't matter. Maybe since God created the cycles of life, He understands when we feel depressed or crabby or anxious. And maybe He still wants to embrace us—no matter our mood, what season we're in, or how many brownies we ate last night.

CHAPTER EIGHTEEN

In Search of the Fair Fight

WHENEVER TOM AND I GET TOGETHER WITH MY sister and brother-in-law anymore, playing pinochle has evolved into a kind of compulsion. Suddenly the four of us find ourselves sitting around the table and someone is dealing the cards.

> *I'm normally a good loser. But we all have our limits.*

Kathy and I usually cream our husbands at the game. That's because pinochle does not rely solely on luck, but also on skill and intelligence. The other night, however, the men must have concocted some kind of an elaborate cheating scheme. While my sister and I collected worthless nines, Tom and Sam racked up double pinochles.

I'm normally a good loser. But we all have our limits—

especially when playing against poor winners. Tom insisted that he wasn't fiendishly smirking and purposely trying to provoke me. But we managed to turn the game into an all-out marital brawl anyway.

I've noticed it's become more popular these days to admit that even Christian couples fight. I'm relieved to know Tom and I aren't alone. But I still worry that other couples who love God don't squabble the way we do.

I hear that they have "fair fights," a concept Tom and I are struggling to grasp. We try to imagine how these spouses manage to sit down, calmly take their mates' hands, and lovingly inform them that they are incredibly irritating.

Having close friends helps. Sometimes they tell me stories about their own spousal spats and I feel less guilty. But rarely do they include the gory details. People, I've found, want to know about others' family feuds but are too embarrassed to admit they are themselves prone to adolescent tactics.

This must be why thousands of people paid millions of dollars last year to watch on-screen husband and wife Michael Douglas and Kathleen Turner literally kill one another in *The War of the Roses*. I guess even the most cat-scratching couple would feel compatible after consuming that one.

Maybe Tom and I should have seen that movie (we never did) the night after our popcorn fight. I had just fixed a huge bowl of popcorn when Tom made a remark I was sure would wound my soul forever (I can't remember now what it was). In retaliation, I turned on the sarcasm because I know that makes him crazy.

It worked so well that Tom grabbed the bowl of popcorn out of my hand and flung it across the room. White, fluffy kernels cascaded everywhere, covering the floor and the couch. A few pieces came to rest gently atop the TV.

Tom stormed off to bed, and an hour later so did I. I left the popcorn mess for him to clean up the next morning at 6 A.M. before he went to work.

At 8 A.M. I awoke to find the kids at the foot of the bed jumping up and down with excitement about our "decorated" living room. Nathan thought it was Easter.

"Stay out of there," I told the boys. "Daddy did it. Daddy will clean it up."

Every time I came downstairs that day I got a new shock. It's hard to adjust to one's living room looking as if an Orville Redenbacher blizzard had struck. As the time approached for Tom to come home, I almost lost my nerve about leaving the mess for him. So I went to church. Maybe that helped because when I got back my husband was neither packing his clothes nor foaming at the mouth. He was still in his suit and tie, humbly vacuuming up the last of the kernels.

He looked at me. I looked at him. We both burst out laughing.

Tom and I are still pursuing the ideal of the "fair fight." And I think we're catching on, although we've simplified the guidelines a bit: no throwing popcorn, no winning at pinochle by more than 2,000 points, and no fighting that doesn't later lead to making up. After all, that's always been the best part.

We try not to get too hung up on this being "fair" business. We figure, as long as we still care enough to get really mad—it must be love.

CHAPTER NINETEEN

The Fuss About Fido

SOME PEOPLE DON'T MIND SOUR SMELLS, SCRATCHED sofas, and ruined rugs. And some people think I'm cruel— just because I've failed to purchase for my boys a Fido, a Spot, or even a Fluffy. Yes, you heard it right. My children are growing up pet-deprived.

One of my friends, who is especially sorry for my children, has four cats. "Cats are so nice," she told me emphatically the other day—just before she jumped up from the couch to chase one of her furballs off the kitchen counter and away from her thawing hamburger.

When my friend sat back down, I kindly reminded her that she's paid more for her cats in vet bills than she did to have her children. And the last time one of her kitties contracted a nasty case of worms, it lost its stomach and deposited a live sample on the backseat of her car.

"Okay," she said, defeated. "But what about a dog?"

What about dogs?

My mom and stepdad's dog immediately came to mind. A sweet slobbering bulldog who has permanently stained their carpet with his drool and has been known to make people faint with his gaseous emissions.

Still, Noah and Nathan think that getting a dog would be paramount to Disneyland. And still, my husband and I are dead set against Spot. We have more than reasonable concerns—but ones that Dick and Jane never addressed in their books.

Proverbs 12:10 says, "A righteous man cares for the needs of his animal." So who would follow our Fido around, helping him to be discreet about the by-products of his private functions? Who would be held responsible when our dog broke into the neighbor's garbage can and decorated the street with its contents because he hadn't been fed for four days?

My children answer such questions with a resounding, "We will, we will!" When Spot first came, they probably would. But after they got tired of scratching his tummy to make his leg twitch, after they learned to hate the smell, texture, and even the look of dog food, and after scooping up oh-so-many presents out of the front yard, wouldn't Spot start to be a sore spot?

It's not that I'm completely hard-hearted. One day Nathan came running into the house and yelled, "Chad got a new puppy, Mom! It's soooo cute." He folded his hands up under his chin and rubbed them together, his cheeks flushed pink with excitement. "I want one, too, Mom!"

That night I couldn't get the picture of Nathan out of my mind. I told Tom, "Maybe we could have the joy of giving the kids a puppy, and then in a couple weeks, when they weren't looking, we could take it back..."

And then it happened. An older woman who babysits our boys was given some fish by a friend who moved. One night when we stopped by she excitedly pointed out the tank and fish. "You can have it if you want!" she told Noah and Nathan. "It just needs to be cleaned, and it'll be great!"

The kids jumped up and down, elated, while I peered doubtfully through the orange spongy slime that clung to the tank and obscured the fish. "Well, I don't know…" I said. But deep down, I did know. To refuse a dog or cat was one thing, but to refuse *free* fish would be beyond cruel.

The fish were no problem. We only had to spend nearly twenty dollars and two hours at the pet store figuring out what new equipment they needed in order to stay alive for more than a day. When we got home I realized I was about to plunge into the utmost depths of parental sacrifice. Somebody older than eight needed to clean out the tank and change the water.

Later, I proudly declared to all my pet-owning friends and relatives, "We have pets now!" But somehow, the fish didn't seem to impress them. And after watching them swim five billion laps around their tiny tank, my boys became unimpressed as well.

"Do they sleep?" Noah asked. "Or is this *all* they do?"

It wasn't long before talk of Fido resurfaced. Nathan's birthday is in three weeks. He already has the obligatory bicycle and the toybox is overflowing. His heart's desire is a puppy.

I'm worried that I'm slipping. Surely, a puppy would stink up the house, chew holes in our shoes, piddle on the floor, and bark at our closest friends. Then again, there are Nathan's big blue eyes. And Noah, whose more mature demands for a dog have begun to wane in the face of such ongoing deprivation…

Three weeks later… He wore a blue ribbon around his

neck at the party. When he wobbled across the kitchen floor Nathan couldn't believe his eyes.

His name is Fido. I told Nathan, "Fido was just a joke name. You can't name a cocker spaniel Fido!"

"But look, Mom!" he said. "He already knows his name. Fido! Fido!"

Of course the puppy came running.

And of course I will regret this. Later.

CHAPTER TWENTY

The Long Way Home

LAST NIGHT, MY FRIEND AND I RAN AWAY FROM home. Debi wanted to escape a checkbook that wouldn't balance and a husband who was unhappy about it. I just wanted to be anywhere my kids weren't.

We drove off with no destination in mind. Sometimes it's more important to know what one is leaving behind than where one is going.

> *We turned up the volume on the car stereo. But nothing is loud enough to drown out God.*

We ended up in a small Italian restaurant on the far side of town. In a back corner at a quiet table, we had one of those deep-water conversations. The kind that have a life of their own. The kind where you wonder what you'd do without this friend and you cling to the fact that you and she are so much alike.

As we talked, it became obvious that a premature mid-life crisis (we're too young for the real thing) had set in upon the two of us. We began to count our sacrifices and weigh our commitments. We set our marriages, goals, and children up on the scales—and the costs struck us as high.

Romance, we agreed, is hard to keep alive while fighting with one's husband over who should flip the handle on the running toilet. Dreams are difficult to foster when time and money won't cooperate. Children are hard to love when they act selfish, sarcastic, and ungrateful.

Eventually our discussion drifted back to the beginning. How we'd married, had babies, set up housekeeping, and tried hard to become what God wanted. Back then we were so sure what that involved: dedication to husband, children, home, and church.

Recently these ideals have felt as faded and worn as the red-checked tablecloth our elbows rested on. We shared our yearning for something new and exciting. We confessed to each other how the world's call sounds so loud to us lately, like an ambulance siren in the night that you're sure must be parked just across the street.

I hear it in the morning when my boys fight over who gets to look at which cereal box. For Debi, it gets loudest in the afternoon, when naps won't be had by her stubborn preschooler.

Around the dinner hour, it can be heard even above the family clatter. It screams at us as we stare at raw hamburger in our frying pans. It yells about how there's got to be something better than this.

We sat in the restaurant for hours, until the waitress' smile faded and a boy with a broom appeared. When we left, we joked about driving to California, never to return to our families again. But instead we settled for a winding back road, the long way home. We turned up the volume on the car stereo—loud enough so that our kids would have covered their ears, so that if our neighbors could hear they'd wonder if we'd adopted a teenager.

But nothing is loud enough to drown out God. Not when He speaks from the inside out.

So I finally leaned my head back against the headrest and asked Him what He thought. Were Debi and I awful? Were we missing His plan for us as mothers and wives? Were we just selfish?

Relief flooded me when God seemed only to smile at my questions. And as we drove through the night, I felt that He understood my hunger for more of life. I thought I heard Him make promises to me about a place of passion He'd help me find; how out of the ordinary in our lives, He could erect something truly extraordinary.

Debi dropped me home around midnight. I hugged her hard before we said goodbye, then walked into my shadowed house and gazed at the scattered toys and tired-looking furniture. Standing there in the semidarkness, I realized peace and passion have more in common than I thought—and I'd never want one without the other.

I climbed the stairs to bed slowly. As I passed my boys' bedroom, I paused to hear them both snoring. I couldn't decide who was loudest—until a minute later when I crawled in bed next to that same sound amplified ten times.

As I snuggled next to my husband, suddenly the world's call didn't sound half as loud. I decided I'd run away again sometime soon. But whether I take the long way or the shortcut, all my roads lead home.

CHAPTER TWENTY-ONE

The Dirt Where Love Grows Best

I HATE DIRT. BUT DIRT AND I HAVE COME TO KNOW each other well. Last week I helped haul ten yards of loam (a pretty word for dirt) from one spot to another.

Tom and I have been landscaping our backyard—for four years. It took a year to ponder the task, a year to put in new sprinklers, and a year to build the deck. This year, we added "good" dirt to the "bad" stuff we already had. Somehow it all looks the same under my fingernails.

As much as I dislike dirt, my boys love it. So do their friends. It seems any healthy kid can smell a pile of dirt from a great distance. The day the heap of soil appeared in my backyard, so did the entire neighborhood population under four feet tall (tiny tractors and shovels included). You couldn't have dragged them off to Disneyland. The little ones cried when we had to haul away their holes.

Still, I know I'll have the chance to get intimate with dirt again. It's unavoidable when you landscape . . . and when you visit a pumpkin patch.

For nine years, Tom and I have resisted the sane urge to buy a perfectly clean pumpkin in front of the supermarket. Instead, we drive to a nearby farm and pile into a hay-filled tractor along with twenty other families in search of a filthy experience. At the last second the farmer always lets a few more (like thirty) people squeeze aboard. Only later do I notice the person sitting on my lap is not someone I know.

Invariably, we choose a sunny day for the trip. Yet invariably, it has rained five inches the day before. That's when I learn anew the other word for dirt—mud. Noah and Nathan have a talent for finding it. They dive for the seats up front where the tractor's wheels spin 'round and 'round. Splat. Splat. Splat.

In just a few minutes my boys bear an uncanny resemblance to the kids on laundry soap commercials—the ones that show children getting as grimy as possible while their unconcerned mother watches with a smile. (She is confident in her detergent. She is also an actress.)

Standing there in the mud, watching my family from a distance, I see them more close-up than ever.

Soon, we jump off the hay wagon and immediately scatter across the field. For the next half hour the quest for the perfect pumpkin is paramount. Our squash has to be just the right shape, color, and size.

Amid the search I notice something. All the pumpkins are roundish and orange, with a green handle on top. Since they all look the same, why is none of them the right one? I know that in a couple of months we'll experience the same phenomenon trying to pick out a Christmas tree.

Resigned to this, I'm first to give up on finding the perfect pumpkin. I settle for an oblong one with a few facial scars. Then I go grab an apple off a tree by the road. It's almost too sour but I eat it anyway, crunching and scouting for my family. I spot my husband, a mile out, still serious about his pumpkin. I see my children bent over intently, their unzipped jackets flapping about them like bird wings. And it is always the same. Standing there in the mud, watching my family from a distance, I see them more close-up than ever.

The return trip in the tractor is usually twice as cramped because of the pumpkins. I am careful to sit on my husband's lap. He is careful to hug me. Meanwhile, the boys dive for the front row of box seats again. They spend the ride getting re-splattered and arguing over who picked the best pumpkin.

Back at the farm, while we wait for our pumpkins to be weighed, we sip hot apple cider and grin at each other. I decide Noah and Nathan look cute in dirt. They decide to trade pumpkins. Then, our cheeks red and shoes caked with mud, we head for home.

As we drive through leafy tunnels of auburn and gold, it occurs to me how grimy the van is getting. Somehow, this time, I don't mind. I decide that maybe there is a good kind of dirt, the kind you don't have to haul. The kind you find in the autumn, in the middle of a pumpkin patch. The kind where family love grows best.

CHAPTER TWENTY-TWO

The Kindest Words

LAST YEAR TOM AND I RESOLVED OURSELVES, almost happily, to a Christmas without relatives. Tom had only one day off from work, so we couldn't make the usual six-hour drive to my mother's.

But then the phone call came.

They couldn't imagine Christmas without us. My family would move the traditional bash to my sister's house, a midpoint between us and the rest of the clan. They were willing to travel the three hours to meet us halfway.

Since Tom had already been up since 2 A.M. that morning, I drove so he could sleep. But why did I imagine my husband might doze with his wife at the wheel on a snow-packed road?

He watched me drive. I watched him watching me drive. He kept saying, "Stay in the grooves! Can't you feel the tires aren't in the grooves?"

I offered him the wheel repeatedly. But he'd decline, say he was too tired, and *pretend* to go to sleep. Somehow we made it to my sister's alive—and still married.

As we greeted the brood, I recalled how a month ago at

Thanksgiving, I'd felt a growing tension amongst the siblings in my family. The clincher had come at dinner. I was about to declare a certain music tape my favorite when my brother broke in with, "Isn't that tape horrible? It was the first tape I ever threw away."

My sister noticed the division as well. How can four people who grew up in the same house turn out so different? And so, on Christmas Eve, after the kids were in bed, she proposed a new tradition—an affirmation hour. Taking one person at a time, she explained, we go around the room and let everyone else tell that person something they appreciate about them.

Strange how nine people can squirm in unison. I gazed at my family in dismay. My mom and stepdad, my three siblings, and their respective spouses. Could I think of something positive to say to each one? And what would they say to me?

Then I noticed my stepdad asleep in a recliner, his book lying open on his lap. Surely he would balk and save us all! But my mother nudged him awake and someone else said, "Hey, we are starting with you, Dad." And before he knew what was happening, he was being told how much his cooking and selfless giving in the kitchen was appreciated.

Our affirmation "hour" turned into three. My normally nonverbal stepfather became a sincere motormouth of goodwill. And my qualms passed as well. Here were struggling humans like myself. People who'd tasted of flattery, but had rarely feasted on true affirmation.

My sister and I were surprised to discover how much we appreciate each others' husbands. Later we had to laugh when we realized we'd said basically the same thing to both of them: "Thank you so much for loving my sister (I know I do, but how could you?)!"

At first, my husband was reluctant. This wasn't his idea of a dream evening. But when he told his brother-in-law he'd been like a father to him, I was shocked to see him swipe at tears. And when it came time to affirm his groove-missing wife, he broke down and cried. Which made me cry, which made my mother and sister cry, too.

Later my mom caught me in the hall. "You know, the best part of tonight was Tom," she said, with a happy sigh. "I have always known he loved you, Heather. But I had no idea..."

We finished at 1 A.M., passing around kleenex and hugs. We felt like we'd been in a movie or a dream. Had this really been us? It was so late! And we hadn't even started to open presents. But everyone agreed—the best gifts had already been given.

Our family is like many families. We grew up with conflicts, trying to get along as best we could. We became a broken family, trying to graft in different parts. But that night we discovered we share a cracked, miraculous wholeness that has nothing to do with our own efforts.

It has everything to do with Christmas. With the One who couldn't imagine life without us. The One who came to meet us more than halfway. The One who keeps making His strange appearance among us, ignoring our wretchedness and saying kind, true things.

We all got shocked last Christmas. We knew He loved us. But we had no idea...

CHAPTER TWENTY-THREE

These
Pricey Pebbles

WANT TO BUY SOME ROCKS? I HAVE A VARIETY spread across my dining room table at the moment. They're getting my lace tablecloth dirty, but never mind. These are important rocks, gathered by my son and his cousin who's visiting as part of a child-switch with my sister. (Why do I always get the younger set?)

Anyway, the rocks are reasonably priced. For twenty-five cents you can purchase a black stone of the sort easily found in most gravel beds. But these kids aren't dumb. The prices go up as the rocks increase in size and novelty. For seventy-five cents, you could splurge on a genuine piece of petrified wood.

The planning and pricing took place last night. I forced the entrepreneurs to bed at 10 P.M., but not before Nathan asked me to set an alarm for 6 A.M.

"We need to get up early to think," he said. "We're worried Chris (the five-year-old next door who contributed a few rocks) is going to want all the money."

I told him they could think better after 9 A.M., and absolutely not before 8. They went to bed in the same bunk, whispering how they would spend their impending fortunes. Nathan had his mind set on a motorized car. Micah was planning to buy all the candy in an entire store. How will I break it to them?

—The rocks?
Someone decided they were
worth their weight
in little boys.

Maybe I should just be thankful it isn't pies. Last summer the neighborhood kids got together and picked buckets of blackberries. I got nominated to bake the pies, since I only write and don't really work like other mothers, leaving me lots of time for this kind of thing.

The pies sold for one dollar a slice or four dollars for an entire pie. It was a smashing success. The kids each made a couple bucks, the neighborhood got warm blackberry pie after dinner that night. I got heatstroke, purple hands, and came out ten dollars in the hole.

But before I start to sound bitter, back to the rocks. I woke early this morning to think about them, too—not because Chris will want all the money but because I know there won't be any. Even now they're setting up the stand out front.

I call Nathan inside.

"Hon, I think it's great you're going to sell rocks. But what if no one wants to buy them?"

"They will, Mom! I know they will. And if grown-ups won't, my friends will."

His friends who have followed him inside and are feeding off his fervor all nod heads in agreement.

I am outnumbered.

"Your rocks are worthless," I want to say, but don't. "You will make fools of yourselves!" What will the neighbors think when all their children come running home to break open their piggy banks so they can buy the Harphams' rocks?

"Nathan," I finally say, "I know you think your rocks are valuable. But they're only valuable because you think they are. Really, they aren't worth anything."

Upon hearing this, his face falls. His friends begin to frown at me and I can tell the pie thing is long-forgotten.

Fortunately, I have a brainstorm. How about lemonade? A chorus of whines goes round. But after I offer to buy the cups, make the lemonade, and help with the sign, they suddenly all get very thirsty and they're sure all the people on the way home from work this afternoon will be, too.

The rocks? Never fear. Someone decided they were worth their weight in little boys. I bought the entire set for a flat ten dollars. I really couldn't afford to. But then again, I couldn't afford not to. Someday these rocks will remind me of whispers in bunk beds and of cousins conspiring to be rich. Right now they remind me that what's common and worthless on the surface can become priceless, if only someone thinks it is.

Could this explain why God bought pebbles like us at the exorbitant price of His own little boy? I guess He couldn't afford not to, either.

CHAPTER TWENTY-FOUR

Slippery Risks
for Sale

SEVERAL DAYS AGO MY MOTHER CAME FOR A VISIT. Before she left, you might say she was all wet. She would say I was.

Tom and I took her to our local swimming pool with a long, winding waterslide. We urged her to try it, telling her what great, safe fun it was.

She hesitated, reminding me that she's never even jumped off a diving board.

I wasn't shocked. My mother's always been shy, and never much of a risk-taker. Her idea of a risk is to drive past a garage sale without stopping.

But daughters have powerful manipulative skills with their mothers, and I am no exception.

Before she could change her mind, Tom hurried her to the top of the slide. When her face turned white just before takeoff, Tom tried to reassure her. He said she could go as slow as she wanted. And he reminded her that no one had ever flown out of a waterslide—or at least not this one in particular.

All we can figure is that she must have doubted this. She

must have decided the safest thing was to lie flat, toes pointed, and try to avoid ejection.

I watched from the bottom. But my mother thundered down that slide so fast I almost didn't see her. You have to understand that my mom is not a small woman. She is 5′ 7″, and as she puts it, "has eaten her share of leftovers."

Yet who could miss her wide-open mouth, her shocked expression? When she shot out the end, her glasses, which she'd carefully tucked inside her bosom, came flying out. In fact, the slide had to be shut down so the lifeguards could help my mortified and now half-blind mother find her spectacles.

I felt bad. But I had learned at an early age that life isn't worth living without taking a few risks. And sometimes people need a little prodding. If you're lucky, they'll thank you. If you're not, make sure they can't find you in the crowded pool.

I got my first lesson on risking when I was five. A nine-year-old neighbor girl wanted me to drop another boy's toy gun into the mailbox that sat kitty-corner from our house. I had no qualms about doing this girl's dirty-work, but I told her I wasn't allowed to cross the street.

"Why don't I just carry you, then?" she said with confidence. "That way, you won't *really* be crossing the street."

Well, that sounded good to me.

So I got the kid's toy gun and dropped it in the mailbox. But on the way back, my accomplice accidentally dropped me upside down on the pavement—my third set of stitches that summer.

That's the problem with risks. Not all risks should be taken, and not all prodding should be listened to. This is what my mom said back then, and also when she found me at the pool, hiding in the kiddie section.

Usually the risks we *need* to take aren't the kind that chance a stitch or two to our head, anyway. They're the kind that risk a blow to our pride. Like a ride down a slide. Or a romance. Or admitting an unattractive truth about ourselves. In fact, some things are impossible to gain without risks: experience, love, honesty, adventure.

My mother must be learning the same thing. It's the only explanation I can fathom. Would you believe that after she recovered from her traumatic trip down the slide, and after she forgave me, she announced she wanted to try it again?

"You're kidding!" I said, incredulous.

"Only this time," she said, "I'll sit up, hold onto the sides, and *go down slowly*."

Of course, my mom fell flat onto her back as soon as she shoved off. And for all of her frantic gesturing and flailing, she couldn't manage to sit back up again.

I stood at the bottom of the slide waiting for my risk-taking mother to blow forth. And for the first time in my life, I asked God to make me more like her.

CHAPTER TWENTY-FIVE

Passing On
the Good Things

SOMETIMES I WORRY ABOUT WHAT I'M PASSING on to my kids, especially in the area of basic life-coping skills. I have a hard time remembering things, even little things, like where my child said he was going. Or where I parked the car.

*E*ven as I
pondered my son's question,
I heard a familiar echo
in my own heart.

The other day, my son Noah forgot his conference slip and called me from school to bring it. I'd already brought lunch money and a math book that week. When he got home, he told me how he informed the secretary at school, "I got this forgetting thing from my mom."

"Oh, really?" I asked.

"Yeah," he answered. "And then she asked me if I got anything good from you."

I waited, hardly breathing.

"I told her I didn't think so," he said sincerely. "Did I?"

After I finished laughing and weeping, I wracked my brain. Something good . . . but even as I pondered my son's question, I heard a familiar echo in my own heart.

As a young man, my father earned his master's degree from Rutgers University. He had a nice family, a good-paying job. Life looked promising—until he developed drug problems, then mental illness. My parents divorced and my dad spent the rest of his life wandering in and out of mental hospitals, missions, and halfway houses.

Growing up I struggled to deal with issues surrounding my father's sickness. On one hand, I longed to identify something good with my dad. But what good could come from being this man's daughter? I silently voiced Noah's question, afraid of the answer.

When I was twenty-three and my father forty-seven, his illness led him to take his own life. And the question grew louder. My younger brother, Jimmy, heard it, too. One night he called my mother and kept her on the phone for two hours.

"Tell me about my father before the divorce, before he got sick," he pleaded. "Tell me all the good things about him, Mom."

She did. And now my brother—who has our father's looks, voice, even the same name—is not afraid to be his father's son.

Throughout his life, my dad had a habit of recording his thoughts on yellow legal pads. It helped him cope. Often, he would mail me long letters stuffed in large manila envelopes. But because of his wild scrawl, they were usually illegible. I always threw them away.

I didn't start writing until after my dad died. At first, I didn't make the connection. Then one day as I was wildly scrawling in my journal, I noticed my enthusiasm rendered my handwriting almost illegible. And I knew I'd found something good.

Last week, my husband came into my den with a shoe box I hadn't seen in ten years. He'd been cleaning out the garage when he caught sight of it. The box was full of letters I'd saved from childhood, including one from my father. My hands trembled as I opened it, the only letter left. My father wrote it during a short-lived recovery period. I was eleven at the time. He said he'd written me once already that day, but had forgotten what he did with the letter. He pointed out that I seemed to have a way with words. He was dreaming he could pull his life together, so he could send me to college in the East someday, and he wanted to be there with help.

Last May marked the five-year anniversary of my father's death. He never pulled his life together the way he dreamed. I never made it to college. But today my father showed up in a shoe box with help.

When I tucked Noah in bed, I told him I thought he got his love of reading and writing from me. And somehow, he managed to get Grandpa Jim's beautiful blue eyes through my brown ones. Then I reminded him that God is his Father. And ultimately, every good gift comes from Him.

Later, lying awake in my own bed, I asked God to tell me all about Himself again. All the good things. Because sometimes I forget. And because I really do want to be my Father's daughter.

CHAPTER TWENTY-SIX

What Begins with "M"?

SOME TIME AGO, NOAH'S SUNDAY SCHOOL CLASS did a craft project involving magnets. In preparation, the teacher asked the kids, "What has six letters, begins with 'M,' and picks things up?"

Only a few of the kids guessed "magnet." Most of them thought the question was too easy: "Mother!" they chimed.

I wish I knew what picture flashed through Noah's mind at that moment. Was it Mom scooping up his and little brother's dirty clothes off the bedroom floor? Was it Mom collecting crayons off the staircase as she threatens to throw away the next small toy her vacuum sucks up, mangles, then rejects?

Noah shrugs his shoulders.

"I don't know, Mom. You just pick things up."

This must mean his image of me has matured since the time he told his kindergarten teacher: "All my mommy does is watch her computer and take naps." I remember frantically trying to reason with him, "But Noah, what about the laundry and dinners and dishes and story times?"

"Oh, yeah," he said. "I missed that stuff."

I shudder to imagine what Nathan is telling his teacher about me.

I hope she doesn't mention mothers for a while because last week I quit acting like a magnet. I didn't pick up anything. Except the flu. I let toys lie. I let the newspapers scatter. I didn't even pick up the towels off the bathroom floor.

The problem was neither did anyone else. The messes mounted. My flu hung fast. By Sunday, I'd changed my mind about ever wanting to be a wife and mother. And the realization that it is now ten years too late did little to console me.

I'd spent the better part of the afternoon brooding in my bed, nestling these and other irrationalities when the phone rang.

It was my mom: "Hi, honey!"

Did she have to sound so cheery?

We talked chitchat for a moment. She rambled on about the plants in her yard and her latest garage sale find. Then suddenly she switched gears.

"Are you really okay, Heath? I was sitting having a quiet cup of coffee and I kept thinking, 'How's my girl?' And I had this strong urge to call you."

That's when I realized that even three hundred miles away mothers still pick things up.

So I poured a bunch of things out. Things I wasn't sure she'd understand, things that somehow reminded me of awkward talks we had years ago. I'd stare hard at the pattern of bumps on her bedspread, while she'd fumble through grossly inadequate explanations about adolescence, boys, and "changes."

Only this time instead of a bed to talk over, we had only the phone. The boys have become men. And the changes that I'm concerned about on my body are stretch marks from babies, not the blossoming of puberty.

So why was I surprised when everything I spread out in front of her, she simply gathered up and held close? She didn't seem shocked by the selfishness I can't seem to shed. She understood my secret struggles. She even confessed to me some of her own.

I guess it's easy to miss all that picking up a mom does when you're little. But it's also easy to miss once you think you're all grown up.

"I forgot that I had you, Mom," I told her. "I forgot that this mother still needs her mother."

She sounded glad I'd remembered. Glad to be needed.

After we hung up, I dried my tears, abandoned my bed, and made my way downstairs. I straightened the living room and put the cushions back on the couch. I opened the blinds. I even hummed.

Nathan noticed. "Are you done being sick, Mom?" He looked hopeful.

"Yes, honey," I told him. "Mom feels a lot better."

His blond head bounced and small arms reached for me. I heaved his forty pounds to my chest and he wrapped his legs around my waist.

Who knows. Maybe I'll get lucky. Maybe Nathan *will* tell his teacher, "My mommy picks things up."

And maybe someday when he's all grown up, he'll understand that she will never stop.

CHAPTER TWENTY-SEVEN

On Sacred Ground

THE TALL ONE ON THE LEFT IS TWENTY-EIGHT. The less-tall one is ten. They waited for the sun to set a little, since it was a hot day. This is a first for both of them. The father has never taught his son to mow. The son has never been taught. They walk side by side behind the mower, sharing the handle, moving in harmonic steps across the yard. From behind, their bodies are shaped exactly the same, except one is smaller. The father talks loudly over the roaring mower. The son listens intently....

"Don't ever ride over rocks. They could fly up and hit you. Don't ever put your hand near the blades. Don't go too fast or too slow. Let the mower guide you...."

The father knows this is hard work. He has pushed a mower over this same yard for years. He's aware how heavy the bag of grass can get and he's familiar with the monotony. He knows what he cuts this week will grow back again the next.

But the son thinks this is fun. He's too young to know the truth: What seems like play now will feel like hard work later. After he's mowed the lawn several Saturdays, he'll begin to object.

When they finish, they come inside to wash their hands. I hug the son, even though he doesn't care to embrace his mother right now. I philosophize, too. They think they simply mowed the lawn.

"This is sort of like your Bar Mitzvah," I say, "if you were a Jew."

"What's that?" the son asks.

"It's like a rite of passage," I say. "It's what happens when a Jewish boy turns thirteen. They have a ceremony to celebrate his becoming a man."

"I'm only ten," he says. "And I'm not Jewish. But does this mean you'll treat me like a man when I'm thirteen? That means I get to drive the car..."

Even after it's been mowed, our lawn is still the ugliest in the neighborhood. It's full of holes and bare spots. This is because it's a corner lot and the best yard for kids to play baseball and football on. It's also because we're the only parents dumb enough to allow our yard to be torn up this way. The football does the worst damage, since the boys play, rain or shine. When it's muddy, clumps of wet grass get ripped out.

*I go outside
to view the lawn. Long
diagonal sections mark the paths
they took, paths my son
will soon repeat alone.*

Often, even when our kids aren't home, a delegate is sent to knock on our door. Usually, one with freckles and a hopeful face. "Mrs. Harpham? Can we play football in your yard?"

I say "yes." I can say no less.

The sounds of their playing float into the house. There are shouts, commands, cheers. Sometimes, I hear tears. They all pause, check for damage, and comfort the victim. "Hey, there. You all right?" (Who says boys can't be tender?) If nothing's been broken and no blood is involved, the next play is called.

Sometimes, I watch them from a window. I think, "You're getting muddy! You're going to get hurt! You're risking your neck with each tackle!" But I never say any of this. I'm not sure why. Maybe I sense their time is short. And what feels like play really is this time.

For now, I convince my son he can't drive until he's sixteen and becoming a Jew won't help. I go outside to view the lawn. The grass looks smooth and cropped in the dusk. Long diagonal sections mark the paths they took, paths my son will soon repeat alone. I notice the bare spots are even more visible now.

The neighbors probably feel sorry for us. We have no landscaping, no raised flower beds—they'd get in the way. We have no hope of golf course grass, only of holes, clumps, and mud. But we do have this: Little boys play here on their way to becoming men. That's when I realize I'm standing on sacred ground—and our lawn is even holier than the neighbors might think.

CHAPTER TWENTY-EIGHT

Rats!
It's Thanksgiving

I'D BEEN STUMPED ABOUT THIS HOLIDAY COLUMN for weeks. A friend suggested I write something funny about Thanksgiving. But when was the last time something funny happened to you on Thanksgiving? Some years it's hard enough just to find something to be thankful for.

This year I'm thankful, in a roundabout way, for the kitty on my lap—in spite of her gas. But I can't explain about Rachel the cat until I explain about Rachel the rat, her predecessor.

This is not a long story. It will only seem that way.

Nathan's dad got him a rat for his eighth birthday.

"Cute little Heidi," said Nathan.

"It's a rodent," I said with a shiver.

Tom's only defense was that the pet store told him rats made better pets than gerbils or hamsters. "They don't bite," he explained. But the pet store failed to inform Tom that while a hamster can scurry, a rat is truly fast. You can't always catch, or find, a lost rat.

You know where this story is going. First chance, Nathan takes Heidi to his friend Brett's house. Nathan loses Heidi in Brett's house. Nathan is upset. Brett's mother is more upset.

Brett's father buys a live rat trap and begins to stay up every night after his family has gone to bed—trying to catch the rat.

When two weeks pass and it appears Heidi will spend eternity terrorizing the neighbor's house, I go to the pet store. I let Nathan pick out another rat. Rat number two is Rachel. She is littler than Heidi.

A few days later, Brett's father shows up at the door. He proudly displays an apprehended Heidi. "She had only two nights left," he says. "And then it was a death trap." I think I spot a gleam in his eye when he says this. Perhaps life takes on a new meaning when one is stalking a rodent for one's frightened wife.

Life also takes on new meaning when you own not just one, but two rats. Nathan quickly determines, however, that not only are the two great pals, Heidi is mothering Rachel.

But eight-year-olds have been known to misjudge these things. One week later, Rachel's tiny form lies stiff and cold in Nathan's outstretched palm. Poor Rachel. Poor Heidi—a murderess. It's a week before Nathan can forgive and love the only rat he has left.

A few nights later, I'm lying in bed, 3 A.M. A lot of noise tells me a burglar is in the house. The noises stop after a while, but I leave my light on. Then I see it. A flash of gray and pink. Heidi on the loose—again. She noisily worked off the lid to her cage while standing on her food dish.

I break it to Nathan gently.

"How come none of my pets want me?" he asks, tears streaming down his face. "They all run away or die..."

Three days later, Heidi is still a fugitive. I tell Nathan we're going to the pet store to get a live trap. Once there, he races over to watch the kittens play behind a glass wall. He gave up asking for a kitty a couple years ago.

"Go ahead," I say, smiling. "Pick one out. That's why we're here."

"Really?"

It's too much for him, too good to be true. He picks out a gray and white short-haired tabby. He calls her Rachel, in honor of the deceased.

A week later, Heidi is apprehended in Nathan's underwear drawer. One of Nathan's friends happens to be visiting. This friend happens to call his mother and ask if he could have a rat, cage, food, and all—for free. I know this mother can hardly say no. And that she will hate me. I don't much care. It's a rat eat rat world, you know?

So there you have it. Not much of a holiday story? Think again. Think of Nathan's face when I told him to pick out a kitty. Think of Rachel's relief at being picked. Think of all the surprises God springs on us daily that are almost too good to be true—but are. Now I'd call that something to celebrate.

CHAPTER TWENTY-NINE

My Way
or I
Won't Play

I KNOW GOD LAUGHED THE DAY KIM'S FAMILY moved in next door to ours. That was seven years ago—back when I lived a rigid, orderly life. I had beds made, sinks scrubbed, and kids dressed by 9 A.M. Almost nothing happened in our home that wasn't planned.

And Kim definitely wasn't—planned, that is. My new neighbor showed up on my front porch in her bathrobe every morning. She could chat longer than I could pretend to listen. She didn't seem to care if either of us ever got around to clearing the breakfast dishes off the counter.

I hated Kim . . . then we became fast friends.

Friendships are strange that way. Sometimes God brings us a friend who grates against us, just to change us both. Kim taught me how to live with less Lysol. I taught her to put away cereal boxes before noon. Today, we seem to have traded places completely.

My mother used to worry I wouldn't be able to make friends. I was a "my way or I won't play" type of kid.

From age two to six I lived next door to a naive little blond thing who let me manipulate her continually. Threats worked wonders on Shelly. She would sacrifice her favorite

stuffed bear, best Barbies, even the right to control Ken—
all for me to stay and play.

But one day something clicked inside Shelly. She refused
to hand over a red teapot, even after I threatened to go
home. I was shocked. Standing in her backyard, scattered
with toys, I finally resorted to, "If you don't give me that
teapot, I'm going to throw all your toys over the fence."

She wrapped her arms more tightly around that prized
possession and said nothing.

*T*he amazing thing
was this: My first friendship
survived the worst in me.

One by one I picked up the toys then looked at Shelly.
She'd shake her head "no" and I'd toss the thing over the
fence into the sticker bushes behind her house. First a doll,
then a broken top, a shovel and bucket, her favorite stuffed
bear. . . .

When all the toys were gone, I stomped home. Somehow my mother got wind. I had to apologize. Then my
mother, Shelly, and her mother watched while I climbed
through the poking sticker bushes to retrieve the goods.

The amazing thing was this: Shelly still liked me after
that. My first friendship survived the worst in me.

Today, I have my friend Debi. We go walking almost
every night and I have often wondered which we exercise
more—our legs or our tongues. It is amazing what a dark,
quiet walk around our familiar neighborhood will bring

about. Sometimes we laugh so hysterically the neighbors peer out their windows and wonder about us.

Other times, Debi and I are serious. Life weighs down on one or both of us, and the subject is not chitchat. It's stuff like the certain sin I've been struggling with lately. One of those kind you fight, kick, and shove away, but all the while still chase after.

Debi's been sympathetic. She lets me gather my toys around me—my excuses, my Barbies, my theories, my way. That is, she did until last night. That's when she said some hard things to me. Things that have to do with my selfishness and pride.

A part of me wanted to storm home. Or better yet, lash out and start throwing her virtues over the fence. Who was she to say? I longed to argue the point. Except for one problem. She was right.

Debi said something else, too. How much she loved me. Her voice cracked and her eyes watered as she spoke, and I knew friendship had survived seeing the worst in me. Again.

I went home and wept, and some of the sin broke under the weight of love. I thanked God for the Shellys, Kims, and Debis in my life. I thanked Him for friends and enemies, and the best who are both.

CHAPTER THIRTY

Leaving Alone Behind

THE OTHER DAY I LEFT MY SON BEHIND. BUT THEN, I was threatening to leave Noah behind when he was three years old. "Get in the car," I'd say. "Time to go bye-bye."

He'd frown at me, shake his head no, and then walk away.

We both knew the routine.

"Get in the car right now," I'd call after him sternly. "Or I'll have to leave without you."

He'd fold his arms. I'd start the car and begin to drive away. He'd come running after me, crying hysterically. I'd stop the car and open the door for him to climb in.

If this was a test, I'm not sure who passed it. Maybe we both did. He proved he was capable of risking that I'd drive off without him. I proved I was capable of letting him think I might. At some point before he was five, he gave up the game.

Who'd have guessed he'd pick it back up at age eleven?

A few days ago, the boys and I were on our way out of town. As usual, we were running late. When I started to pull away, I noticed Noah hadn't cleared a pile of weed debris off the sidewalk like I'd asked him to. I slammed on the brakes, angry. I ordered him to get out of the car and do it while we waited.

Instead, he began to tell me about some chore that Nathan hadn't done. I lost my temper and began yelling at him. Noah got out of the car, yelling back. "I'm not doing it," he declared. "I'm not *even* doing it." And then he walked away, headed toward a field at the end of our cul-de-sac.

Stunned, I asked Nathan to clear the sidewalk while I waited. When Nathan finished and got back in the car, I drove off. I could see no other way. But six years have changed a lot. This time, Noah didn't come running after the car. And this time, I didn't stop and wait for him.

I went to the drugstore to fill a prescription. I got gas. I took my time. I fumed. I clenched my jaw. I wondered what he was doing. Sitting on the doorstep crying? Would he go to a neighbor's and say, "My mother went out of town and left me for three days"?

When I pulled up at home a half hour later, feeling guilty, Noah wasn't in sight. I unlocked the front door and found him sitting on the floor watching TV. He'd jimmied a back door. I told him firmly to get in the car. We drove in silence for about ten minutes.

"So what were you going to do?" I finally asked. "Did you think I wouldn't come back?"

He shrugged his shoulders. He had a plan, he said casually. He was going to find all the change in the house and return the empty pop cans. He was going to play Nintendo for a while, and then he figured maybe he'd rollerblade to McDonald's for dinner.

All I could think to ask was, "Were you going to wear your helmet when you rollerbladed to McDonald's?"

He said he was.

I apologized for yelling at him. He apologized, too. And then we agreed on a punishment. Farther down the road, I reminded him about when he was three and wouldn't get in the car until I started to drive away. He grinned, remembering. "I always knew you wouldn't really leave me," he said.

"I know," I said. "But you wanted to make sure."

Two thousand years ago, God left His Son behind too. But while I left Noah to scare him, God left His Son so we would never feel alone. And while we collect petty change and scheme for our survival, God is there all along, ready to make us sure, preparing to take us home.

CHAPTER THIRTY-ONE

Sibling Chivalry

AT THIS VERY MOMENT, THEY'RE GETTING READY to come tell. One is trying to patch things up. "I said I was sorry!" The other is still sobbing as he makes his way up the stairs. In a moment, I'll be called upon to sort out a ridiculous litany of events, place blame correctly, and banish "who started it" to his room.

If you have more than one child, you already know what I'm talking about. Experts call it sibling rivalry. But rivalry sounds too chivalrous to me, too much like something solvable. I've tried that. Recently, I forbade my boys to speak to one another—at all—for three days. I considered it a great success. As long as no one spoke, no one argued.

I was reminded of how my mother used to say, "I can't wait until you have kids. . . ."

I thought she was excited for me. Now I realize she wanted revenge. And now I know why. It wasn't unusual for my mother to come home from work to find my brother, Jimmy, and me hollering, chasing each other through the house with butter knives, or trying to pound down one another's doors.

One of my favorite sibling torments involved the empty area underneath the stairs to our basement. It was possible to crouch beneath the steps and as my brother was coming down, just as his back went by, jump out and yell. If I was lucky, he might wet his pants. If I was really lucky, my bedroom door would hold.

A lot of our fights had to do with food. My mom always bought boxes of Ding Dongs for us to pack in our school lunches. But for some reason, we'd often come up a few Ding Dongs short. Eventually, a silver wrapper would turn up under a couch cushion that a sibling had sat on yesterday, constituting an all-out scuffle.

Food is big stuff for my kids, too. Yesterday, Noah ate the last bowl of Nathan's favorite kind of cereal again. "On purpose!" Nathan shouted.

Don't these manufacturers know better than to even include a last bowl? Don't they realize children all over the country are ripping each other's hair out over the last ounce of Trix?

As a matter of fact, I've noticed most kids' fights arise out of the concept of fairness, which is ironic since we parents taught it to them. Whose turn is it to sit in the front seat of the car, to play Nintendo, to pick out the ice cream?

Last night, Noah, Nathan, and even Noah's guest, Jeff, argued about saying grace. It was actually Nathan's turn, but last time Nathan had a guest over, I'd suggested Nathan say grace. So now Noah should. But Noah insisted it wasn't his turn. Finally, I asked all of them: How would you feel if people sat around and fought about who had to talk to you?

While they all tried for possibly the first time in their lives to put themselves in God's shoes, I said grace, even though it wasn't my turn.

That same night, I decided to put my foot down about Nathan's recent habit of sleeping on the floor of Noah's bedroom.

"But I want him in here," Noah pleaded.

"Why? Earlier you couldn't stand him," I pointed out.

"I can't," he said, smiling. "But I promise we won't talk."

I know, I thought. *You'll whisper all night, like my siblings and I used to do.*

Later my brother called me long distance, out of the blue. He wanted to see how I was doing and to tell me he loves me. For some reason, I thought about the stairs. I wondered if he remembered, but I didn't ask.

I could hear his own kids fighting in the background. He apologized. It sounded like war, alright. But somehow it sounded a little like peace, too. Like home. As if rivalry and chivalry are two sides to the same door. As if the door I prayed would hold shut, God held open forever instead.

CHAPTER THIRTY-TWO

When "B" Is as Good as "G"

MY FRIEND KIM SAID NOT TO TELL ANYONE THIS. But I figure by the time you read this, it won't be a big secret anymore. In fact, it may be a live, kicking, screaming being by then. If not, it (he or she) will be too large to hide under Kim's clothes, anyway.

The phone just rang. It was her. Do you think she senses what I'm writing about? Maybe I should be coy, just in case.

The contents of the parenthesis in the first paragraph is particularly important, seeing as how Kim already has three of the sex that begins with "B," instead of "G."

I still haven't given anything away, have I?

So Kim especially wants one of that other sex—the one I have none of, either. Of course, this makes me very sympathetic to Kim's plight. In fact, the last time something like this happened to Kim, I prayed with her for months, debating all along the benefit of fervent pleas in such a case. Wasn't the deed done? Would God really change His mind?

Thanks to an ultrasound, we found out that God wouldn't. And we had time to let go of the "G" word before the actual gift arrived—yes, with one of those "B" indicators attached.

Kim named him Jacob. He is a year and a half old now. And if you sing the music from Barney's TV show, he smiles and begins to rock from left to right. "I love you, you love me . . ." When their family comes over, we grown-ups follow him all night with our eyes, our hearts . . . babystruck I guess you'd call it.

But here I've gotten carried away, which is surprising for me. I usually pretend a certain callousness toward babies, perhaps since I've never given birth to the gentler sex.

How baby Jacob won me over, I'm not sure. Even when I rescued him from the jail of his stroller to carry him at the mall, he returned the favor by belching up baths of sticky white substance on my shoulder. Once, I had to buy a brand-new shirt to wear home because he'd so thoroughly soaked the one I had on.

*O*ne can't help but
*think a girl would understand
such things better. Issues of
scent, timing, decorum.*

One can't help but think a girl would understand such things better. Issues of scent, timing, decorum.

For example, the other day Kim gave Jacob his first doll (to help prepare him for the new baby). He hugged and kissed her as directed, and then promptly tossed her into the back of his dump truck where he apparently plans to keep her.

If all this sounds sexist—that's because it is. I believe in the differences between the sexes. I believe some generalities may be made, with exceptions of course. Even my boys experience exceptions to their usual generalities which shall remain unmentioned, since I love them.

Take the other night. Granted, it began with a paper airplane flying into my room at high speed. A girl would have slipped a pink card with flowers on it under my door. But inside the airplane, if you followed the directions to unfold it, was a coupon. The invitation read: "Good for some free dances downstairs with the radio."

This is about as close to having girls as I will ever get. So I laid aside what I was doing to see what was happening. Sure enough, a dance show awaited me. The boys had fetched strings of Christmas lights from the attic and shaped them into a huge heart on the floor. I took a chair. I smiled. The music began.

That's all I can tell you, however. Like Kim, my boys insist on some secrets. And like all good mothers and friends, I try not to reveal too much.

Besides, some things speak for themselves—such as the opened-mouth kisses Jacob gave me the other night, or his latest attempts to say my name (or is it to rename me?). Deep down I think I'm glad to know there isn't a prayer in the world that could change a "B" to a "G." I guess God's as babystruck as me.

CHAPTER THIRTY-THREE

I Hear
Him Calling
My Name

YESTERDAY IT HAPPENED AGAIN. I ANSWERED the phone to hear my friend Debi's agitated and breathless pleas: "Come quick! I have to take Kyle to the hospital...."

A few minutes later, I walked into what has become a familiar scene. Debi in the bathroom at the end of the hall with four-year-old Kyle in her arms at the sink. Blood spattered her white T-shirt, but she seemed more calm than usual.

She wordlessly lifted the wet rag on Kyle's face to reveal a deep but fairly short vertical cut on his eyebrow. He was crying and sobbing, "I don' wan siches, I don' wan siches...."

A couple months ago, a distracted Kyle rode his bike into a parked truck, sending him to the hospital for stitches above his lip. Weeks earlier, a bit of a Christmas candy cane had to be removed from his eye at the emergency room. This time, a trip to go brush his teeth somehow resulted in a collision between his face and a doorjamb.

On each occasion, Debi has called me to help. I find Kyle's blankie, locate Debi's purse, and help them load into the car. Then I take her older son home with me.

When I was Kyle's age, I had a lot of stitches, too. One time, I was spending the night with a friend when I fell off the bed and cracked my head on a nightstand. Since my parents couldn't be reached for a medical release, her parents took me to the hospital and made me pretend I was their daughter, Kimmy. I'll never forget lying under a blue paper sheet while the doctor and nurse repeated, "Now Kimmy, don't cry, Kimmy. It'll be okay, Kimmy. . . ."

I didn't mind the stitches half as much as I minded being called by someone else's name.

Today, I asked Debi how it went at the hospital. She said Kyle was very good. Before they stitched him up, she gave him permission to get upset. He could yell or scream or cry all he wanted, she said, but he *had* to cooperate. He *had* to hold still.

"He started out with controlled protests," she confided, "like, 'I don't like this.' They escalated to 'That hurts! I want my mommy!' Finally he was screaming hysterically, 'Mommy! Make them stop this right now!'

"That was the hardest part," Debi said. "The nurse told me I should keep talking to him. So I was trying to comfort him . . . but then my *own* voice started to break."

I knew exactly what Debi meant. When my son, Noah, was two years old, he drank a bottle of allergy-control Visene. He had to be tied down so they could pump his stomach and it was hard to tell who was more hysterical—him or me.

Noah has long-forgotten what Visene tastes like. But I wonder what Kyle will remember of his traumas. The sound of his mother's voice breaking above him? How his mother's friend helped find his blankie? Somehow, these many trips to the emergency room will become a small part of who he is.

> *Worst of all, Mom can't always save you from pain, even though she'd like to.*

Meanwhile, new truths are sinking in. Kyle's getting the idea that life can be dangerous. Bad things can happen without warning—especially when you live recklessly. Worst of all, Mom can't always save you from pain, even though she'd like to.

As I walked home from Debi's, I thought about past wounds of my own, both emotional and physical. So many hurts have been healed, the pain used for growth, the scars barely visible now. But as I continue to live, I keep getting hurt. Sometimes it's an accident involving another person. Sometimes I've simply been reckless.

I can't wait for the day when I finally become whole and God wipes every tear from my eyes. For now, I think I hear His own voice breaking somewhere beyond the sound of my protests. For now, this is all I remember of life: God was calling me, moment by moment, by my own name.

CHAPTER THIRTY-FOUR

Beneath Golden Arches

I SAW A COUPLE OF MIRACLES THE OTHER DAY. Not your ordinary kind of miracles, but the kind that make you wonder what else you're missing. The first miracle took place downtown Manhattan at a McDonald's on Nassau Street. And I think I'm the only one who witnessed it.

I hadn't visited New York since I was a teenager, so I immediately noticed this wasn't your average West Coast McDonald's. I've yet to visit a McDonald's in Oregon that features live entertainment, customer seating on two levels, and a well-stocked gift shop filled with the restaurant's paraphernalia.

The place was packed with New Yorkers. Some in suits and ties, some in sweats—and some in clothes too weird to categorize. Unlike me, they didn't seem to find it unusual that while we wolfed down value meals, a musician plinked out a tune on an elegant baby grand piano.

I felt sorry for this guy. He's probably here chasing his dreams, I thought. Maybe he's trying to make it on Broadway. In his off-hours, he auditions and gets rejected. At his day job, he plays piano for an audience more absorbed in their Big Macs than his music.

And then it happened. Some black children who had been eating upstairs began to hang over the balcony above me and call out to the man at the piano. They wanted him to sing something. They waved, trying to get his attention.

Finally he noticed them. And then he smiled. Not a performer's smile, but his own, real smile. He seemed to chuckle to himself and make a flash decision. Then he sat up straighter and flew into a jazzy number, singing, "New York, New York..."

He put all he had into it. And for the length of the miracle, nothing else mattered. He forgot he was in a McDonald's in Manhattan on a gray, drizzly day. He forgot he might get rejected again that night. He forgot his audience was composed of a few kids with catsup smeared on their shirts.

He smiled at his fans while he sang. Let's forget, he seemed to be saying, that you're black and I'm white, that you're young and I'm older. Let's forget that my life is hard and yours will probably be harder. You're here and I'm here. And isn't there just something good about that?

I doubt a truer, greater connection was ever made between an artist and his audience. I wanted to throw money. Or at least clap wildly. But as is often the case with these kinds of miracles, they seem almost ordinary at the time. So I finished off my fries.

The second miracle I witnessed took place on a bus. I noticed one woman immediately, because she was so fussed up. Perfectly manicured fingernails. Expensive jewelry. Designer clothes. I could tell she was very wealthy and I wondered if she was a snob.

Just then, an old, dented brown car rumbled up alongside the bus. There was a family in it, with five children jostling in the backseat. One scruffy-looking boy with a dirty chin was hanging out the car window. He stared blankly at the faces on the bus, his gaze finally settling on this woman.

I expected her to flinch, look away, or pretend she didn't notice. But instead she smiled warmly, lifted her hand, and waved at him. A look of wonder crossed his face. The boy, startled but grateful, waved back.

I had gone to New York expecting the worst. For days I clutched my purse in fear. I'd heard the warnings. Murders. Muggings. Unfriendly people. Racial tensions. But nobody warned me about the miracles.

No one warned me that even in New York, chasms can be crossed. One rich life might be willing to wave at a passing poorer one. A struggling musician might lose himself for a moment, having been found by a few true fans.

But then, who would have guessed at the greatest miracle of all? That a star could be discovered in a place as ordinary as a manger. That God would be willing to be born a man. And that by His birth a great chasm would be crossed, leaving us startled but grateful forever.

CHAPTER THIRTY-FIVE

No One's Naked Here

I TRY NOT TO LOOK OUT MY KITCHEN WINDOW anymore. Not because it needs to be cleaned, but because the view has changed. The window looks out on the same set of houses. But Debi doesn't live in one of them now. Last winter, Debi's husband, David, got a job as head pastor of a church in Washington State. Debi and I had been talking about the possibility of them moving for months. As we walked our usual route, noting signs of winter, we sensed God bringing great change to both our lives. But we didn't know whether to long for or fear what came next.

The changes turned out to be harder than either of us imagined. For me, they seemed an impossible loss. As my best friend planned to move away, my husband decided to move out. Tom wanted to find a new life, perhaps an attempt to make up for freedoms he forfeited by marrying young. As he gradually lost his faith in God and us, our marriage resisted all efforts at resuscitation.

It's impossible to explain the failure of a marriage (especially when you're a Christian) or the huge void Tom left behind. Maybe that's why I miss so many small things: watching him dig around in his drawers trying to find clean socks in the morning—and the way he never got mad about it. I miss the way we'd make dinner together sometimes, alternately cooking and sitting on the kitchen counter, talking. And then last night I thought of my boys and winced when I heard a neighbor boy call out happily, "Daddy! Daddy!" at the sight of his father's car in the drive.

Tonight, as I look out at the house where Debi used to live, I miss her whole family, perhaps another way of missing my own. I miss catching her husband, David, wearing his funky flannel nightgown in the morning. I miss attempting conversation with Debi over a cup of chocolate coffee amidst children's commotion. I miss calling out before (actually just after) I barged into their house, "Is anyone naked?"

Once, Debi's son, Kyle, confronted me before I got to the door and with five-year-old authority informed me, "No one is naked, Heather."

A few weeks before Debi left, she and I went out to our favorite Italian restaurant with the red-and-white-checked tablecloths. We tried not to talk about my divorce or her impending move. We didn't want to cry. But somewhere between my salad and pesto, I couldn't help blurting out, "It would seem easier to die."

The other day, Debi sent me a card. All she wrote was a quote from Frederick Buechner: "You can kiss your family and friends goodbye and put miles between you, but at the same time you carry them with you in your heart, your mind, your stomach, because you do not just live in a world, but a world lives in you."

Later, Debi told me she was thinking of Tom and me when she wrote that card. As the holidays came and went I missed our old neighbors and, even more, Tom. But the fact that I miss them means I didn't "miss" them. I knew them. And now I carry them inside me, a world of memories and moments that will always be part of my life.

In the end, Kyle was *right*. No one's naked here—even though I've never felt more exposed. God has clothed us, picked us up, and is moving us on. Surely, He carries us around in His gut, unable to forget His great love.

The view from here has changed a lot. But my vision is still the same: "I will not die, but live and will declare what the Lord has done" (Psalm 118:17).

CHAPTER THIRTY-SIX

A Sister's Labor

MY SISTER IS HAVING A BABY THIS MORNING.

As I drive my boys to school down streets lined with blossoms, my mind is a state away in a dimly lit labor room. I grip the steering wheel tighter. I am overwhelmed with thoughts of my sister.

I know too well the agony she is feeling. The gratefulness for the cold, sweaty bars on the bed. The irrational anger toward an onlooking husband who gets to sit back and watch (they call it coaching).

But I also remember the exuberance. The thrill of seeing that small, wet head. The shock of having another being appear out of your own. There is no joy like it. No pain more intense. I wipe my hands on my jeans. How can the two co-exist?

As we near the elementary school, my boys begin to argue in the backseat over something of major unimportance. I ignore their feud, hoping they'll work it out. My thoughts fly back to my sister. Wasn't it just yesterday she and I were arguing in the backseat of our car?

Now that I have kids of my own, I suspect we drew that imaginary line down the backseat just so we could fight

153

over it. Or maybe we drew it because lines are hard to find in life when you're little. Like the line between parental love and hate. Or the line between good times and bad times.

During our childhood, my sister and I had our share of both. Some days we ate ice cream and went swimming at the local pool. Other days we choked down creamed tuna on toast and our parents got divorced. But we never asked life questions. And we didn't attempt to separate out the good from the bad.

"Mommy, why are you crying?" Noah interrupts my thoughts.

"Oh, honey." I smile at him, unsure of the answer myself.

"I was just thinking about Aunt Kathy," I said. "She's having a baby right now, you know?"

He looks confused. Children don't understand that certain relatives are so much more than that. Or that tears can be cried for lots of different reasons.

I pull up at the school, and before he hops out of the van, Noah gives his brother a quick hug. I'm amazed how quickly their quarrel was forgotten. How quickly they are friends again.

I watch my oldest son run into the school building, swinging wide the heavy metal doors. He looks confident, ready. Today something good will happen. He will probably ace his spelling test. Something bad will happen, too. Maybe one of the kids will tease him about his name, "Noah, where's your ark?"

Somewhere inside, he must know this. And yet it doesn't stop him. And I can't help wondering how long this lift in his step will last.

A few more years, perhaps. And then he will get to know life better. He'll encounter heartaches and rejections. Responsibilities he doesn't want. At some point, he'll wish again for the carefree times, the tag days. And no doubt, he'll try to draw lines down the backseat of life, separating out the good from the bad.

I pull the van out past the crosswalk patrols and head for home. The spring sun feels warm on my face through the windshield. Warmer because of how cold winter was. I whisper up a prayer for my sister's labor. And for Noah's, too.

I pray that after this life hurts him, he'll be able to forgive it. That someday his own tragedies and triumphs will begin to blur together. And that he will be able to embrace all of life.

Who can separate the pain from the joy? I don't think I want to try.

Once at home, I sit and wait for my sister's phone call. I anticipate the sound of her voice, both ecstatic and exhausted. I know she will gasp about how terrible her ordeal was and how she never wants to go through it again. And then a moment later she'll exclaim that it was the most wonderful experience in the world.

Who can separate the pain from the joy?

I don't think I want to try.

This morning my sister is having a baby.

CHAPTER THIRTY-SEVEN

Eyebrow
to Eyebrow

THIS WEEK IT'S OFFICIAL. NOAH HAS ONLY THREE inches to go. He gave me a gloating grin as he handed me proof—the results of his latest health screening at school. It seems they were kind enough to list, along with the news that he doesn't have scoliosis, his exact weight and height.

Doesn't the school realize such information should be kept private from kids like mine? They should've known he'd come home and take a victorious spin on his mother's office chair and then ask, "So how tall are you again, Mom?"

I grabbed the paper from my son and told him to quit smirking. "Hmmm," I said, pretending to look over the sheet. "So you don't have bad eyes."

"Look at my height," he demanded.

"Aaah," I said, trying to sound casual. "So you are only three inches away . . . But three is a lot," I pointed out. "It'll be *years*."

I guess I shouldn't blame Noah for trying to be as tall as me, since his dad's height of 6′ 5″ must seem unattainable at this point. Even so, I'm getting a little tired of the game.

Noah comes up almost every day to measure his height against mine.

"You are still only at my eyebrows," I tell him each day. "Just like yesterday you were at my eyebrows."

I blame others for how it started. Noah might never have noticed that I don't lean down to kiss him anymore, or that we can reach the same shelves in the kitchen cupboard. But it seems that wherever we go—church, or even the grocery store—someone is bound to call out, "Boy! He's about to pass you right up, isn't he?"

Don't these people realize how fragile and desperate the man-child ego can be? My son latches onto such comments as if inches equal equality of some kind, as if his life will somehow drastically change forever the moment we're eye to eye.

Perhaps in his dreams fireworks will go off in the cafeteria at school to commemorate the occasion. Or maybe all the students will rise to salute The Tall One. At the next student assembly they'll make an announcement: "This week Noah Harpham passed his mother up."

In the meantime, his first year of flag football hasn't lessened his obsession with height. A few nights ago when he came home from practice, he came strolling up to me and stood real close. At first I thought he wanted to give me a sweaty hug. Then it hit me. He wanted to be close, alright. But it wasn't affection he was wanting to measure.

I shoved him away. "Where will it end?" I asked him. "When I'm looking up your nostrils?"

"Yeahhh," he said, obviously liking the thought.

Saturday we all went to his first football game. I was surprised by how well he played. He knew just what to do. He was also the tallest kid on his team. And it seemed to me, standing there on the sidelines and shielding my eyes from the sun, that he got taller each time he carried the ball.

It also seemed to me that he looked just like his father. Ah, yes—his father. How could this be? Wasn't it just yesterday I was a teenager watching his father play football? Wasn't it just yesterday, too, that I was telling his father, "We're going to have a baby"?

When Noah came off the field at halftime, I patted his damp back. It was a broader back now beneath my palm. And when I tried to brush his wet hair off his forehead, he shirked away. Of course, I told myself. He is big enough now to handle his own hair.

After the game as we left the field, I walked beside Noah. I had casually laid my arm across his shoulders when another player's father noticed us. "Boy, he's about ready to pass you right up, isn't he?"

My eyes stung a bit for some reason. I could feel my son's body straighten a bit beneath my arm. "Yes," I said, but with a smile this time. "It'll be any day now. Any day."

CHAPTER THIRTY-EIGHT

Going
Beyond Cool

I WAS WALKING THROUGH THE COLLEGE CAFETE-ria the other day when I passed a booth full of sweaters for sale. These weren't your average sweaters, but very sweatery sweaters. "Hand-knit in Ecuador," the vendor informed me, eyeing my conservative blazer that, previous to my return to college, I'd been proud to wear for three years.

"But, of course," I answered back, trying not to appear surprised. The sweaters not only looked hand-knit, they looked as if they might baa at any moment. Balking at being dyed purple, perhaps?

I bought one. I put it on immediately and finally made a few friends. "Oh, I love your sweater. Did you get that here?"

Since returning to school a few months ago, my whole world feels a little off-kilter. I am a mom, sort of, a writer, sort of, and now a student, sort of. The challenge is doing all these things well at the same time and feeling at home in each part.

Take the sweater vendor. He was counterculture, had frizzy, long hair, and wore psychedelic clothing left over from another era. I used to feel uneasy around such people simply because they looked different. Now I sit next to them in class each week and ask to borrow their pens.

I'm also learning a lot of new things at school that aren't on any tests. Like last night when I left on my car lights, drained my battery, and didn't have any jumper cables. I learned it's highly unhip to ask a man for help. I'm supposed to feel some feminist shame or something. I can only hope no one saw me: "Yes, please, sir, mister, that's my car over there...."

I've also learned that if something's bad, it's "chew" (as in, "Wow, that was chew"), that it's important to wear flannel at least once a week, that it's uncool to say "cool," and it's also uncool to go to church, which is unfondly referred to as organized religion.

As collegiates see it, to say that God as I understand Him happens to be Jesus Christ is definitely not cool (oops) at all. It is better, I'm told, to have a more blob-like kind of God; a vague, undefined, force-like being who is part of you, me, and the entire world. Call him what you will. Better yet, call her what you will.

But how does one become intimate with an aura? How is one redeemed by a universal inner good? I understand part of the problem. It's scary to give God a personhood, to believe in something specific. Too many specific people have hurt these students. A force feels safer.

Maybe they're right that God is a ridiculous prospect. The problem with God, I'm figuring out, is that He is love. These students don't love their higher power. They get help from their source. So do I. But I'm in much deeper than that.

My Source is no neutral being or mindless mass of energy. He asks me to get intimate with Him. He knows every secret of my soul, every story I've ever lived. He not only holds the entire world together at its core, He cradles all my hopes in His hands.

So even with my new sweater, I don't always fit in at college. I still don't have any flannel or even a hooded shirt. Some days, it's lonely.

I am, however, getting better at making friends. I remind myself that I reflect part of God, and I try to really mean it when I ask the depressed woman sitting behind me, "How are you?"

I admit that reaching out to others (who don't know hoods mess up hair) can feel risky. But it's a small gamble in light of more important truths: Christ died for students and God ain't no blob.

CHAPTER THIRTY-NINE

Never
Miss a Beat

NOAH WENT TO HIS FIRST DANCE THE OTHER night. But let me clear up any misconceptions: This doesn't mean he asked a girl to go with him. It doesn't even mean he danced. In fact, I doubt he heard noises that sounded like music as you and I would think of it.

He went to the dance with his friend, Jeff. It was their first middle school dance. When they came home, I expected tales of torrid romance—or at least of puppy love. "Jeff got punched in the face," was all Noah said.

Jeff smiled. This, apparently, was the highlight of the evening.

"By who?" I asked.

"He bumped into some older kid," Noah explained. "An eighth-grader. But we told the chaperon and the kid got kicked out."

Noah confessed that he hadn't asked any girls to dance. "What if they say no?" he said, and Jeff nodded his head in agreement.

I finally sent them to bed to ponder their evening, what moments they might savor, and what moments they might

regret forever. I, too, lay awake and tried to remember
...and then quickly tried to forget.

The next day I was at Noah's football game and several
groups of girls (this is how they travel) showed up to watch.
As I was walking the sidelines, one of the girls approached.
Big smile, pretty hazel eyes. "You're Noah's mom, aren't
you?"

I remembered Wendy (not her real name, mind you)
from Noah's kindergarten class. She was still a cutie. "Yes,
I'm Noah's mom," I said.

She wanted to chat—about Noah. We talked about the
previous evening, and in particular how Noah didn't ask
any of the girls to dance.

"Maybe Noah doesn't think any girls will say yes," I ventured.

"I know lots of girls who would say yes!" she exclaimed. I smiled.

She went on. "I think Noah is just kind of shy. When I walk by him in the halls and say hi—he says hi real quiet and then looks away."

"Well, don't stop saying hello to him," I said. "I think you're right that he's a little shy."

Looking satisfied, she politely said goodbye and rejoined her friends—armed with what I hoped wasn't too much information about my son. A mother can't be too careful. I could already hear Noah saying: "What did you tell her about me, Mom?!"

Once, I liked a boy who was as shy as Noah. And like Wendy, I was anxious and determined. While I never talked to Jason, much less his mother, I did get a big break once. It came in a musical our class was putting on. We were doing two productions, "Tom Sawyer" and "Hansel and Gretel."

I stood at Mrs. Thorson's chipped black piano, belting out songs with my heart in every note. She had no idea my life was depending on this.

Jason was trying out for Hansel's part and obviously had the best voice. I stood at Mrs. Thorson's chipped black piano, belting out Gretel's songs with my heart in every note. But Mrs. Thorson had no idea my life was depending on this. She couldn't have, because two days later, I got the part of Becky Thatcher.

Sara Sievers, a sweet blue-eyed blond with tiny immaculate penmanship, would play Gretel.

After school that day, I went to Sara. I begged. I pleaded. I appealed to her on the basis that Jason meant nothing to her. She agreed to trade parts and we presented our case to the teacher—leaving out the part about Jason. Mrs. Thorson was resistant. But she finally gave in with the firm stipulation that we could not change our minds again.

The next day she handed out the boys' parts. Jason was going to play—Tom Sawyer! A month later, Sara, decked out in old-fashioned frills, shared a kiss with Jason on stage. I, garbed in a rumpled gunnysack pinafore, sang, "Brother, come and dance with me!" to a Hansel so huge we had to remove the lines, "You're toooo skinny!" from the play.

Jason never did notice me. At some point, I quit noticing Jason. Gradually, I adopted a more straightforward approach to love. I learned that rejection, and risking it, is part of the great dance of life. And that if I manipulate the steps too much, if I get impatient, I might lose what rhythm God has planned to give me all along.

Noah is determined to dance at the next dance. And I am, too. When the time is right, I'll take the chance. And if God strikes the chords, I'll never miss a beat.

Other Good
Harvest House Reading

HONEY, I DUNKED THE KIDS!
by *Phil Callaway*

This collection of captivating tales from the bright side of family life will greatly encourage you, touch you, and keep you laughing! Award-winning columnist Phil Callaway turns life's bloopers and blunders into timeless spiritual lessons for young and old alike. Every story—every page—is rich in wisdom and entertainment. Curl up in your favorite chair and brace yourself for a delightful time!

DADDY, I BLEW UP THE SHED!
by *Phil Callaway*

Through his ordinary adventures as an everyday guy, Phil shares his wit and wisdom on topics as varied as the crazy things kids do, the tender moments between mother and son, and why Dad knows everything. In this lighthearted, and inspiring look at family life you'll recognize your spouse, your kids, your parents—even yourself!

365 THINGS EVERY PARENT SHOULD KNOW
by *Doug Fields*

So your kids didn't come with instructions? Don't worry. These bite-size bits of lighthearted wisdom will encourage you every day of the year. They're funny. They're pointed and they're packed with dynamite advice for raising great kids.

365 THINGS EVERY WOMAN SHOULD KNOW
by *Doug Fields*

There are just certain things a woman should know, and certain things that *only* a woman *can* know. These gems of insight, witty sayings and pithy one-liners will have you thinking *and* laughing at the same time!

365 THINGS EVERY COUPLE SHOULD KNOW
by *Doug Fields*

This little book is loaded with lighthearted wisdom and insight into the hallowed (and often harried) institution of marriage. *Don't yell at each other unless the house is on fire* is just one of the witty, poignant exhortations you and your partner can enjoy together. These maxims will spark fun, romance, and care in your relationship!

365 THINGS EVERY MAN SHOULD KNOW
by *Doug Fields*

Every man should know dirty socks left on the floor cannot walk to the hamper on their own is just one of the many fun and thought-provoking proverbs of manly wisdom you'll find in *365 Things Every Man Should Know*. Tongue-in-cheek wit and sage advice join forces in this lighthearted look at men and manhood.

GETTING THE BEST OUT OF YOUR KIDS
by *Kevin Leman*

Time-tested advice and a healthy dose of humor are nationally recognized psychologist Keven Leman's prescription for great parenting. Dr. Leman offers solutions to the toughest problems parents face and gives practical advice on raising kids from start to finish. This information-rich book also includes a special section on the character traits of oldest, middle, and youngest children and how to adjust your parenting to fit.

Dear Reader:

We would appreciate hearing from you regarding this Harvest House fiction book. It will enable us to continue to give you the best in Christian publishing.

1. What most influenced you to purchase *I Stole God from Goody Two-Shoes*?

   ☐ Author   ☐ Recommendations
   ☐ Subject matter   ☐ Cover/Title
   ☐ Backcover copy   ☐ _____

2. Where did you purchase this book?

   ☐ Christian bookstore   ☐ Grocery store
   ☐ General bookstore   ☐ Other
   ☐ Department store

3. Your overall rating of this book:

   ☐ Excellent   ☐ Very good   ☐ Good   ☐ Fair   ☐ Poor

4. How likely would you be to purchase other books by this author?

   ☐ Very likely   ☐ Not very likely
   ☐ Somewhat likely   ☐ Not at all

5. What types of books most interest you? (Check all that apply.)

   ☐ Women's Books   ☐ Fiction
   ☐ Marriage Books   ☐ Biographies
   ☐ Current Issues   ☐ Children's Books
   ☐ Christian Living   ☐ Youth Books
   ☐ Bible Studies   ☐ Other _____

6. Please check the box next to your age group.

   ☐ Under 18   ☐ 25-34   ☐ 45-54
   ☐ 18-24   ☐ 35-44   ☐ 55 and over

Mail to: Editorial Director
Harvest House Publishers
1075 Arrowsmith
Eugene, OR 97402

Name _____

Address _____

City _____   State _____   Zip _____

**Thank you for helping us
to help you in future publications!**